The Best We Could:
A True Story of the Afterlife and Discovering the Light Within

Julie Richmond

To Mike, my rock.
To my children and sweet granddaughter, my extra blessings.
To David, without whom I would never have known.
To Rose, my other me.

Always Love,
Julie

Author's Note

True Story - This is a true story. Many names have been changed out of respect for each person's privacy. The timing of the events was compressed to facilitate the telling of the story. It has been 12 years between David's death and the publishing of this story.

I considered changing the parts in which I felt I might be viewed as a not a very good person. Then, I realized that by doing that, I once again was choosing to live my life based on others' opinions of me rather than being true to myself. The choices, decisions we make create our identity. Hiding an integral part of me due to fear of others' judgment couldn't truly explain who I am. My journey consumes me; it is me. After so many years of holding it all in, I finally had to let it out. No matter what. I grew up with get over it and move on, with convenient faith, with self-doubt and never wanting to call any negative attention to myself. I can't revise what has happened to me, what has shaped who I am. I had to share all of the 'bad' to help make sense of the beauty in it all. And there's plenty of beauty; that's why you get the truth. No matter what. It was hard for me, but I did it anyway. It's time for me to live big, too.

No part of this book is intended for educational purposes. This story is about my personal experiences. Please keep in mind that no two people experience the same communications from spirit. They are as individual as each of us is. Be open to your own experiences. Trust that they are real as soon as possible rather than be like me and wait ten years before truly believing them. I've always been a slow learner.

What Others Are Saying:

The Best We Could:
A True Story of the Afterlife and
Discovering the Light Within

"Richmond creates a tone that lets us suspend disbelief about David coming back to her, expressed through her confidence in her story and a cautious optimism that we will believe her tale. It adds richness and depth to the story, in the author's understanding that her tale may seem unrealistic to some. But we're invited into her truth, and eager to experience what we hope we could experience for ourselves." Judge, Writer's Digest Self-Published eBook Awards

"Julie has written a deeply moving and inspiring account of life's lessons and the mysterious twists they present -- even after death." *The Best We Could: A True Story of the Afterlife and Discovering the Light Within"* is a riveting must read for those who seek love and understanding -- what this life is all about, and most of all, truth!" Susan Sanderford, Spiritual Medium

"In all the thousands of memoirs I've read, I've never read anything so complex made so relatively simple and affect me so profoundly." Jo Mary Stafford, Author of *Light in the Dust: A Staffordshire Childhood*

"I was most taken with the authenticity and candor of this true story. Understanding the background helped explain the level of grief, and the amazing communications that continued after death, not just to show an earthly love but to help explain the eternal, unconditional love that we are." Amazon Reader Review

"Beautiful recount of how spiritual and earthly worlds intersect. It must have taken a lot of courage to write this book. It's a beautiful and honest recount of the spiritual connection between two individuals that transcends this physical world. It begins from the perspective of an adolescent who is falling in love, filled with yearning and confusion, and moves to a beautiful description of one woman's journey as she learns about the timelessness of love and how the spiritual world and the earthly world intersect. I really loved this book and couldn't wait to find out what happens next to Julie. It is filled with wisdom, love, and some incredible validations!" Amazon Reader Review

"A beautiful and soul-searching book. The writing is solid, and the story follows a smooth and easy direction. What I took away as the main theme of the book, aside from theological differences, is that love transcends time and death. A truly heartwarming story. I applaud the author's courage to be vulnerable and share her story in such a unique and moving way. Recommended for anyone on a spiritual journey wanting to know what other beliefs are out there." Amazon Reader Review

"Intergenerational memoir. I shared this book with my two nieces after I read it because I liked it so much. It is a beautiful story of love, connection, healing and friendship. Most importantly, especially for young girls to understand, it is the story about the wonderful capacity of strength and power that we all have if we are open to it." Amazon Reader Review

"I think this is an important book because it challenges us to think outside the cultural framework of how we experience love and spirituality. It is an emotional book, and I enjoyed her honesty and her perspective." Goodreads Reader Review

Contents

Introduction 1

Prologue 5

PART ONE: Little Kid Lost.....................................8

11 Months Old 8

2 Years Old 9

5 Years Old 9

6 Years Old 10

8 Years Old 11

9 Years Old 12

10 Years Old 13

11 Years Old 15

12 Years Old 17

13 Years Old 18

PART TWO: David, Forbidden Fruit...................20

The First Time 20

Oh Crap. He's Married 23

Mid-Winter Retreat Part 2 - The Next Year 29

The First Letter 31

He's Still – Summer Church Camp 33

Broken Pitcher 37

The Types of Love 39

Mission Work and Jelly Beans 43

Hey Jules 45

Tournament Weekend 49

Embracing Life 55

Let's Dance 61

Mischievous David 64

Faith on the Tower 66

Like a Daughter? 71

Whistling Out the Window 75

No Boy Will Ever Like Me 78

Mike 82

Plans for My Future 83

He Kissed Me. Finally. 87

Gebel Sweetness 89

Feeling Stagnant 92

Field of David 96

Bully Mom 99

A Guitar Promise 103

Suicide and Dreams 105

Come See Me 109

You Mean More to Me 110

It's Goodbye 111

Random times throughout the years... 117

PART THREE: I Want to Die, Too 118

I'm a Grown-Up 118

Flowers for the Living 122

Call Nothing Thy Own 126

I'll Never See You Again 129

Forever 42 130

Rose and Judy 131

So Angry 134

(Not) Wearing My Seatbelt 135

Asking for Signs 136

Hearing God 140

Unsure 141

Understanding Love 142

Giving it to God 144

Understanding 145

PART FOUR: Prove It (He Still Exists) 148

Desperate to Know, Scared to Be Wrong 148

I Want to Be with You 150

My Son Saw an Angel 152

I Never Realized 155

Tigger and More 157

Don't Doubt David 160

Maddie Sees Him 161

Finally Playing His Guitar for Me 164

White Rabbits Everywhere 166

It's a Real Thing 171

Because I'm Here for You 173

Seeing Sparkles 175

Happy Valentine's Day 176

Automatic Writing 182

PART FIVE: What Did You Learn? 185

Peace 185

Lessons in All Forms 187

Blondin/Trust 188

Yes, Lord! 190

Out of My Comfort Zone 191

Balance 195

Caught Up in Purpose 196

David Appears 197

It's in You 204

Come Here 205

Made Up of Light 207

Another Visit 210

About Dad 213

Base Spirit and Angels 215

Part of the Holy Spirit 217

Suicide? 218

How Do I Live Here? 219

The Best We Could 223

Another Little Lost Girl 225

Religion 228

Facing Fear 230

Negativity 232

What Now? 233

About the Author **237**

The Best We Could:
A True Story of the Afterlife and
Discovering the Light Within

Julie Richmond

Introduction

Life - a series of events strung together by days, weeks, responsibilities.

Living - understanding joy and where we come from, knowing peace, allowing the unconditional love within us to spill out into all that we do.

I knew when I saw him the first time playing his guitar and singing I was going to fall hard, and I did. To anyone else he may not have had that effect. He wasn't drop dead gorgeous. Not according to romance book or movie standards, anyway. But according to mine, there was no one better looking. He had brown hair, cut short although it was a little long in front. He'd swipe it off his forehead in a gesture I came to know well. His face was strong; good bones, my grandma would say. I could tell he'd had braces as a kid. His smile, so big, filled his face, reached his eyes. I also came to know that smile well. His nose was…well, it was just a nose. A good one, I suppose. No extra bumps or twists. Not too big or too small. Just right. But his eyes. His eyes. They stood out most of all. His eyes were blue, blue like…like what? Like the Caribbean off Cancun where I'd vacationed with my family the summer I turned 14. How corny is that? Oh well. Clear, bright, big, blue, beautiful eyes

1

topped with extra thick eyebrows that added to every expression crossing his face. I came to know his eyes well, too. And those eyebrows. And all of his many expressions. I learned to tell exactly what he was thinking just by watching his eyebrows. As for his eyes, it wasn't just their color. It was how intense they were. He could see right inside me with those eyes. I could never hide from him, never pretend. I could only be me with David, and the crazy thing about that was that it didn't matter. He liked me. Me. He accepted me in all my weirdness. And I was a strange one, believe me. I never felt like I fit in – with my family, with my friends.

Talk about pretending (and the fact that I couldn't with him), I pretended my whole life. Pretended I was cool, that I was tough, that I liked squealing and giggling with other girls about this or that. I pretended so that I could fit in somewhere. I spent my life pretending until I met David and then I couldn't anymore even when I tried. He didn't let me. He prodded me with his intense gaze until I spoke up and told him my opinions, my feelings, my dreams. He listened and he nodded and he asked questions and totally accepted me. At first, it was disconcerting. I wasn't used to anyone completely accepting me, not even my mother. Especially not my mother. But then I came to trust him. His steadiness. His love. And I knew I'd found that one person in the world who completely complemented me. Not complimented although he did that, too, but complemented.

I won't defend my feelings or my actions even though I often want to. It's part of that insecurity in me that I've always had – never wanting to make waves, never wanting anyone to think poorly of me. But here it is. I'm laying it all out here - the love I shared with someone I 'shouldn't' have. Love we have for each other. Yes, even now. Because you see, he came back to me. Ten years ago, David died. He died. I had to say that out loud many times over the years. David died. Saying it out loud helps to process it, I guess. I had to make it real, concrete. David died. But you know what? I learned something new, something I had only hoped for before. Only his body died. He didn't. Not really. He came back to me, and the best thing about that (besides the fact that he wasn't really dead) was that he still loved me. And he still taught me. Teaches me. It's still happening, so why wouldn't I share? I learned love, real love not romantic love. I learned hope. I learned to trust – God, myself. And I learned to live.

I spent my life before David pretending. Then, for ten years after he died, I pretended again. Oh, on the outside all was well. And it really was. But inside of me, there was always something missing. I pretended that wasn't so, though. I made believe I had it all together.

Thank God, I don't have to pretend any more. No, that doesn't mean I now have it all figured out. It just means that I understand what's real, what's right. I understand who I am and well, if and when I don't have it together, it's okay. I'm okay.

This is not a religious book, no matter that I talk about Jesus and discuss my early upbringing in the church. Instead, it's a discovery of truth, of an enormous, all-encompassing God, and of the seemingly miraculous events that unfolded for me. I was a Christian before I wrote this book, at least by name. When I began experiencing the things I did, I briefly thought I couldn't be a Christian any more. I was wrong.

Through discovery and experience, I learned I am still a Christian. If anything, I'm 'more' of one because I know the peace and love that He brought into this earthly world. I understand the comfort of truly knowing we continue after death. Learning firsthand that life is eternal doesn't negate Christ. To me, it glorifies Him; it honors Him and shows the magnitude of His love. Realizing that whether we call God God or Universe or Source or any other term doesn't take away from the enormity of His (I use the masculine His only because I grew up that way. Read Hers or Its if you want. It's all the same) love. I will not try to convert you in telling my story. I don't really care what you believe except to the point that I would wish for you that in whichever way your beliefs take you, you will know and live love.

Let me start from the very beginning and share with you my journey. Some of this you'll relate to. Some, maybe not. I promise you, though, it's all true. Every bit of it really happened, and it changed me forever.

If you find nothing else here, I pray you at least find hope. Life is eternal. Love is eternal. Prove it, I told David.

And he did.

Listen little Julie. I am but a breath away. You see me in the sun and in the love in your children's faces. I love you every moment. You know what to do. Get the story out. Tell the story. Tell about love. Then. And now.

Prologue

I felt a breeze brush softly across my upper arm. In my dazed confusion that comes in that in between place of awake and asleep, I snuggled up under my blankets a little tighter.

The breeze wafted across me again. This time, I considered the fact that quilts covered me; how did I feel a breeze on my arm?

"Julie."

I heard a deep voice, whispering but firm. Loud enough to awaken me. Rolling over to see what my husband, Mike, might want with me in the middle of the night (no, not that!) I saw that he lay facing the opposite wall, his side heaving steadily up and down assuring me that he was sound asleep and hadn't called me at all.

"Julie."

My heart jumped a little. If it wasn't Mike, who could it be? An intruder? One who knew my name? That didn't make any sense.

Slowly, I rolled over and peeked through the slits of my eyes. Maybe if I didn't open them very wide and it was an intruder ready to murder me, he wouldn't realize I was awake. He might pass me by.

A misty white light glowed, brightening the bedroom. Weird. I knew we'd turned all the lights off. I'd checked three times...at least. I always had to check things in multiples of threes. I hear that's quite an OCD tendency, but oh well. I'm functioning. For the most part, anyway.

It seemed the light in front of me, right beside my bed, condensed. The straggling of light that was spread this way and that came together and began to take form.

"Hi, David," I whispered, as soon as his shape came together enough for me to recognize him. I saw the shimmery outline of an arm reach out, the index finger point at Mike across the bed from me and then slowly press against his see-through lips to indicate he was shushing me.

In my head, I heard him. "Don't talk. You'll wake up Mike. I can hear you this way." His words were thoughts in my head. Distinct, definitely separate from my own. I knew they weren't my own thoughts anyway. I'd tested him enough by making him give me information I didn't know but could prove in the early days when I first started hearing him.

"Hi," I thought at him, and I grinned.

By then, he looked like a real man standing right in front of me. Well, he was a real man, just not physical. Not anymore. His body made of light had come together, concentrated enough so that at a glance anyone else would think he was just a guy standing around in our bedroom in the middle of the night. Just a guy with a little bit of extra light emanating from him, that's all.

He smiled and a rush of memories came flooding through me, a rush of emotions. Every time I felt him, heard him, saw him, it was the same. It was like no time had passed. The 20 years since I'd last physically touched him could just as well never have happened.

Joy filled me, the emotion so strong it took me such a long time to figure out what to do with it. How do you *feel* so much and have no place to put it? How do you *love* someone so intensely only to have them be a wisp of light in the night, unheard and unseen by most of the rest of the living world?

You do it by realizing that it's the love that's real. It's the love that matters. It's the love that transcends this physical world and the spiritual world. Sharing love makes the earth His kingdom, just as heaven is. Love is God. Love is us.

Through the past ten years, I'd learned. David was teaching me - about what life was really about, what love was really about.

It took me a while, but I got there. Am getting there. Turns out it's not about David. It's not about any 'one' person at all and certainly not about two.

I looked back up at my dearest, sweetest friend - the love of my life, but not in the way you might think, not in the way I used to think - feeling the warmth of his smile touch my soul. I thought of how grateful I am, how my journey has been.

Reaching out, I touched the tips of my fingers to his arm. I didn't feel him, of course. If I pushed a little further, my finger would go through the light that made up his arm. I stopped from that, though, imagining how it used to feel, and I smiled up at him.

"Rest," he told me. "You've got lots to do today."

"Everyday," I laughed at him.

He nodded. "True. So get busy."

I rolled away from him, my back to him, and tightened my covers back around me. "Later."

I heard his laugh fade away as he went back to wherever it is he goes and I dozed, hoping for at least a few more minutes of sleep before starting my day.

PART ONE: Little Kid Lost

11 Months Old

I don't remember, thank goodness. My birth mother (my 'real' mother) hung herself after months of battling paranoid schizophrenia. I napped in my playpen in the room next to the bathroom where it happened. My older siblings, Megan and Thomas, played outside completely unaware that at that very moment, our mother was stepping off a chair. Who knows how long it would have taken anyone to find out if it weren't for my bratty brother picking on my sister? She ran in to tell on him as any good little sister would do. I can't begin to imagine what Megan thought when she first saw Mom hanging from a jump rope, chair kicked over backwards, me snoozing in the corner. I do know Mom wasn't dead yet. Megan ran screaming for Thomas; together they raced back in and tried to get Mom down before it was too late. They couldn't do it.

Quiet and calm, in a straight-faced manner that I only later learned was his coping persona, my nine-year old brother called Dad at work. Megan cried in the background. I kept on sleeping.

I'm glad I don't remember any of it.

2 Years Old

Dad married my stepmother in a Brady Bunch-like way. She had three kids; he had three kids. Instead of the idyllic life of the TV family, however, my family functioned differently. From the outside, our lives painted a perfect picture – big house, swimming pool, parents with successful careers, smart and motivated children. While those things held true for me, too, inside I felt differently. I spent the next many years lonely, unsure of myself, wondering why I could never measure up.

5 Years Old

"Uh uh. No, she didn't." I stopped smack dab in the middle of the street. My best friend, Brenda, and I were walking from my house back to hers – four blocks – it was a different time, back before parents drove their kids everywhere. Even at five and six years old, we freely roamed the streets of our neighborhood. Brenda had just told me something I couldn't quite believe.

"It's true," she insisted. "Your mom killed herself. She hung herself from a jump rope. My mama told me so."

I scrunched up my face and peered at her out of slitted eyes. Our mothers had been best friends; I'd grown up with Brenda. She'd never lied to me before, at least not that I knew of.

"But why would she do that?" I didn't really understand the concept. I didn't know people could kill themselves. Why would anyone kill themselves?

Brenda shrugged. "Mama says she had a sickness in her brain. She got confused."

I still didn't understand. I got confused sometimes. Did that mean I had a sickness in my brain, too?

"Daddy never told me about that," I told her. My dad was the smartest person I knew. He would have told me, I thought.

"I wasn't supposed to tell you either," Brenda admitted. "Don't tell that I told, okay?"

"Okay," I promised.

Brenda took my hand and we started walking again, making our way back to her house. I didn't say anything. I could only think about what my friend had just told me. My mom killed herself. That was a lot to make sense of. I wasn't sure if I could.

Later that day when I got back home, I threw away my jump rope.

6 Years Old

I gripped my pencil tightly and concentrated on drawing the puppy. Megan had taught me how to draw one, and I knew if I could make it just right, Mom (we called our stepmother, Mom, from the very start) would love it. I wanted very much for her to love it. Already at six, I knew my mom didn't love me as much as she loved my stepbrother and stepsisters. I realized I couldn't do things as well as they could, that I wasn't as nice as them or as pretty as them. But I wanted to be as good and as pretty. Then, Mom would love me, too.

I added the finishing touches - spots on the muzzle, admired my work, and ran to the kitchen to get her. She followed me back into the den drying her hands off with a dish towel as she came.

"Look what I made for you." I was so proud.

She laughed out loud and went back into the kitchen leaving me standing over my paper looking after her.

I guessed I couldn't really draw after all. It was a stupid puppy anyway.

8 Years Old

"Did you clean your room?" Mom glared down at me, her expression tight and disapproving.

Click, click, click. I played with the clasp of my watch too nervous to look up at her. She terrified me.

"Yes." I mumbled. Click, click.

"What? Speak up." Her sharp voice made me flinch. Click, click.

She stepped toward me. I kept playing with my watch. "What are you doing? Would you quit clicking that clasp? Why are you doing that?" I shrugged and tried to peer up at her to make the eye contact I knew she wanted.

Click.

"Stop it!" Impatient. Angry. "Stop doing that. What is wrong with you? Do you need psychological help?"

"No." I shook my head at her.

No.

9 Years Old

I sat in the principal's office waiting for him to call my dad. I was in trouble, again. Usually, I could slip through the trouble without my parents being contacted. This time, however, I had apparently gone too far. Shoot, all I'd been doing was talking. And talking. I didn't really think it warranted a trip to the principal's office where I not only awaited my dad's disappointment, but I was pretty sure I'd heard mention of a paddling. A paddling! For talking! I guess when you'd gotten your name on the board and then three extra marks next to it as warnings, that wasn't a good thing.

It's not that I set out to intentionally get in trouble each week in school. It just happened. I was a pretty bright kid, but I didn't always apply myself. I knew that because I'd heard the adults saying it. School came easily for me for the most part, at least easily enough for me to do 'good enough'. My problem seemed to be that I could never stop talking.

It's funny looking back. I was very shy and didn't like any attention. Oh, in my room alone at home, I dreamed of positive attention. I practiced being popular, or a pop star, or a famous actress on the red carpet. But in reality, I didn't really want people looking at me. I knew I didn't look 'girly'. I didn't like fashion or Barbies. I wanted to be tough and athletic. I felt so different than all the other cute girly girls. I quickly learned that if I could just make people laugh then when they did look at me, it was okay. If they smiled and laughed, it was all right. And well, if they ever laughed at me instead of with me, I wouldn't really know that…or at least I could pretend I didn't.

And so I talked too much, cracked jokes, and found myself in trouble frequently. This time with my name and three marks, I'd gone too far.

"Julie," Mr. Roberson addressed me, and I looked up, scared and unsure. I really had tried to stop talking. Really. I couldn't respond to him; I was too nervous. And so he continued, "Julie, I spoke with your father. I'm going to give you your swats now, and he said to tell you he'll speak with you when you get home."

I could only stare at him, eyes wide. I was scared of the swats, but I was even more apprehensive about facing my dad, afraid of disappointing him. My dad, with his loving, infinitely patient but firm manner…I hated disappointing him.

10 Years Old

My family went to church every week. My parents participated in everything church-related. Dad stayed involved as a church elder, Sunday school teacher, Dial-a-Prayer speaker, and anything else our church needed. Mom cooked and cleaned for every church meal, served on the diaconate, participated in the women's group, and even sewed the curtains for the baptistry and the cushions for the pews.

They never gave us the option of not going, as I found out very quickly one morning. I wanted so badly to be rebellious. I dreamed of rebellion. When it came down to it, though, I was a wimp.

One Sunday morning, I felt nice and cozy still in my pjs. I did not want to dress up and go sit in church; for one of the first times ever, I considered being defiant.

I threw on some old shorts and a ratty t-shirt and headed downstairs for breakfast. Mom stood at the kitchen sink rinsing juice glasses. She turned to look at me as I walked into the room, her expression changing from pleasant to quizzical and stern.

"Why aren't you dressed for church?" she asked me, her voice harsh. She scared me a little. Okay, a lot. But I had it in my head I wanted to stay home.

"Oh," I said. "I decided I'm not going today." Well, apparently that wasn't the response she was expecting. Her face pinched, her lips pressed firmly together, and she gave her head a slight shake. From that, I knew I wasn't going to be staying home. For one brief moment, I considered going ahead with my planned defiance but after glancing at Mom's face one last time, I thought better of it.

"Go change for church," she said.

I just nodded and went to change. Talking back to my mother never ended well. I wasn't brave enough to push it.

11 Years Old

The Oklahoma spring sun beat down on the back of my neck causing a little stream of sweat to trickle down around and onto my cheek. A little bead hung ready to drip into the dirt. Absent-mindedly, I swiped it with the back of my hand and focused my attention back on the roly poly I had captured. I was waiting for it to open back up so that the guys and I could race it. Yes, that's right. Several of the boys in my class and I each caught little black insects, made a race track in the dirt, and watched them navigate the course in a competition to see whose roly poly was the fastest.

We did all of this on a break from track practice. Having already run the 100 yard dash and, I have to add, beating the other girls, there was time to kill while the relay teams practiced. A group of girl sprinters stood over by the trees casting glances of disgust at us while we crouched down in the dirt.

Courtney, the leader of the snotty girls, yelled out, "Hey Julie, you're getting all dirty down in the mud with the boyyys!" She singsonged 'boys' and made it sound like a bad word. What a creep. I knew she didn't think boys were bad; otherwise, she wouldn't chase them all the time. Courtney just didn't like the fact that the boys liked me. It didn't matter to her that they saw me as one of their own. She didn't want anyone else to have their attention.

I'm sure she never got dirty. Even after running track, her hair always looked perfect, her clothes matched, she never sweat. I always looked like I'd just barely survived a storm.

"Shut up," I called back to her, refusing to look up. I wouldn't let her see my face and run the risk of her discovering I cared what she thought. Lance, the coolest of all the kids, elbowed me. "Let her have it, Julie." He egged me on. I wanted to just ignore her and hope she wouldn't say anything else. The other boys chimed in, though. "Yeah, Julie. Come on. Let her have it."

Grinning at them, hiding my fear, I scooped up several of the roly polies and stepped towards her.

Her eyes widened. "Get away from me," she shrieked as I raised my arm.

I sped up and once I came within less than a foot from her, I launched the bugs directly at her face. Without a word, I turned around and headed back towards the guys who were laughing hysterically, some actually rolling on the ground.

"You are sooooo weird!" Courtney screamed after me.

I didn't look back. Instead, I stood a little straighter, walked a little taller and joined the boys again. We'd have to find more roly polies to race. That was no problem.

"Great job, Julie," Lance praised me. I grinned again, but inside I felt empty. It was no fun to be accepted by the boys by distancing myself from the group I really wanted to belong to. It made me sad, but I was determined never to let anybody know.

12 Years Old

Lisa and I sat in the hallway after having been sent out there by our teacher. Together, we'd managed to disrupt our entire 7th hour history class. We couldn't help it, really. Everything we said to each other was so unbelievably funny (to us and the rest of the class, I'm sure) that we had to keep talking and cracking jokes.

I'd met Lisa earlier in the year. The first time I saw her out on the playground, her legs were wrapped around the branch of a tree as she dangled upside down. Impressive for sure. Lisa was a fine combination of all I wanted in those middle school years - a tomboy who loved climbing trees, playing sports, shooting cap guns but also a middle school cheerleader who had begun to wear (whisper it in awe) makeup to school dances and while cheering for the football team. I don't know how she fit in both worlds, but she did. For that, I was amazed. I never fit in anywhere.

Oh, I had some girl friends but none I was close to. My childhood friend, Brenda, and I still hung out, but she was a year older and so at school we never saw each other. Church was our thing.

I'd found Lisa, though, and school had markedly improved even if we did tend to get in trouble the majority of the days.

"What do you think she's gonna do to us?" I asked Lisa, referring to mad Mrs. Johnson, our history teacher.

Lisa shrugged. "Who cares? It won't be a big deal anyway. We were just talking."

"Yeah," I agreed. "Who cares?" I didn't really mean it, though. I cared. I hated getting in trouble, but

I just couldn't seem to stop it. It was one thing to have everyone looking and laughing at me when I meant them to. It was another to have the attention on me be negative.

13 Years Old

I spent at least half an hour trying to pull my straight, just below chin-length hair back into barrettes. All the girls in eighth grade wore their hair that way, and I wanted desperately to fit in, to feel pretty, and to no longer look like a complete tomboy. Brenda and Lisa had boyfriends, but the boys still considered me 'one of the guys'. I wanted Lance and the rest of the boys I'd grown up with to notice me, as more than a buddy.

I hoped my pretty and popular sisters would notice my hair, too. And my mom, maybe she would notice, see how good I looked, and be impressed. Maybe she might like me better and be nicer to me.

I stuck the last clip in and checked the style out in my mirror. It didn't quite look like Lisa's, but it was close.

Feeling confident at first, I skipped down the stairs and into the kitchen where Mom stood at the stove making dinner, her back to me. All of a sudden I felt unsure, but I pushed away that feeling and stepped into the room.

"Hi, Mom," I said, anxious for her to see my new hairstyle.

She turned around, and laughed. "Who did your hair? You?"

My heart sank. I nodded but just looked down at my feet. She didn't like it. No longer did I feel confident; I just felt defeated. Working so hard to make my hair look pretty didn't matter. I couldn't do it. I simply didn't have what it took to be pretty…and pretty was what was important. Mom made this ugly gaspy sound and turned back to her cooking; I simply turned around and went back upstairs.

PART TWO: David, Forbidden Fruit

The First Time

You ever have one of those people in your life you just totally connect with? You know the person I mean? The one who you think about, the phone rings, and it's them. Or you don't see them for months and when you come together again, it's like no time has passed. Yeah. I'd never had one of those. And then I met David.

It took me months after the first time I ever saw him to actually talk to David. Junior year of high school. I was 16 years old. I played tennis, giggled with my friends about guys, played more tennis, sighed with my friends about guys. I was very deep. Well, as deep as tennis and guys go. I giggled about David after I saw him, too, but I didn't talk to him.

That January, my youth group went to a weekend Mid-Winter Retreat at the same Christian camp site I'd gone to for a week of summer camp every year since third grade. I loved camp. It never bothered me being away from home for a weekend. Or a week. Or more. Being somewhere else gave me the chance to work on being myself without fear of constant comparison and criticism. Whoever 'myself' was. I hadn't figured it out yet, but I came closer to that every moment I spent away from home.

Going to camp gave me a break from the everyday stress I felt trying to be good enough. To feel good enough. Church camp offered me a place I felt safe, a place I fit in, where people liked me just for me.

I made good grades in high school – mostly A's, sometimes a B in math or science. Somewhere along the way I'd begun to 'apply' myself. Doing well got better attention than not. My stepsisters, though, made straight A's. I heard about it regularly from my mother. Thinking about it, my 'real' sister and brother made straight A's, too. I wonder why Mom didn't constantly remind me of their academic success. No matter. I couldn't help but compare myself to my siblings, and I never felt good enough.

Playing tennis, I found success. In fact, I was state runner-up two years in doubles. Second place in the whole state. Twice. I'm not trying to brag, but that's pretty good. Right? Guess what, though. My stepsisters got first at State in basketball when they were in high school. I heard all about that from Mom, too. What I never heard was any acknowledgment or validation of my own accomplishments.

No matter what I did, they did it better.

I spent so much time at home trying to be perfect and exactly what my mother expected from me that when I was away from her judgmental eyes, I acted a little off the wall. Maybe that's normal. I don't know. 'Off the wall' suited me. Silly, loud. Anything that allowed me to keep people from knowing the inside of me, the insecure me. I constructed my wall of protection very early on. It was built with anything and everything unserious. Being criticized or made fun of when I exposed my serious self crushed me. When people laughed at my silliness, well, that was the point. It was okay then.

On Friday, the opening night of the retreat, Brenda and I headed into the mess hall, and that was where I saw David for the very first time. Sitting high upon the mantel of the huge rock fireplace, he sang and played a guitar. He wore a puffy red ski jacket, baseball cap, and white sweatpants. A huge crowd of teenagers gathered around the base of the fireplace and watched, some singing along, some just listening, some talking to each other and not paying any attention to him. I stood at the back of the pack unable to get very close. Even from behind the crowd, I noticed something special about him. He was cute, yeah, with his brown hair sticking out from under his ball cap, his even features and broad smile, but it wasn't only that. He had such energy. Such presence. I couldn't have explained it if I tried. I felt drawn to him. Pulling out my little Sony disc camera, I held it above the head of the guy in front of me, tried to position it the best I could, and snapped several pictures, hoping at least one would turn out.

The entire weekend I never spoke a word to him. Every time I'd spot him, butterflies invaded my stomach and some sort of palsy afflicted my hands. I'd pop off with some loud comment and hysterical laughter to whoever I was with (usually Brenda) and hope he'd notice me and see how fun and witty I was. Yeah, well. That didn't happen.

Shyness and insecurity kept me from approaching him. Apparently, none of the other kids suffered my fate. Crowds of them gathered around him, and no way would I push my way through them. What if I did and then he just looked at me like 'who do you think you are' or 'you're dumb'? What if the other kids said or thought those things? I just couldn't do it. Instead, I enjoyed the rest of the weekend the best I could and found happiness in the times I got to at least watch him from across the room, giggling every time he said something funny. Or even something not funny. I just giggled. I was 16. That was enough for me.

Oh Crap. He's Married

Spring came. A couple of the pictures I'd taken of David turned out, and I'd carried them around with me for the past four months. He served as youth director at another church in a town a million miles away. Or maybe it was just about 100 miles. It was all the same to me. He lived far away. He wasn't one of the kids. I'd never ever see him again. The end.

Brenda and I were at our own Christian Youth Fellowship (CYF) meeting on Wednesday afternoon. Our group met at least once a week usually just hanging out, sometimes doing a Bible study, or whatever. We all liked to be together. A few of the guys played pool. Brenda went to the kitchen area to pull out the cookies we baked from the oven. I stood on my head over in the TV area trying to see how long it would take to make myself dizzy from all the blood rushing down.

Connie, our youth director, sat on the couch watching me. "Let's have a lock-in," she announced.

I swung my legs over backwards instead of forwards and hit hard on the tiled floor. It hurt. I bounced up quickly anyway. "Hey," I suggested. "We could invite David's youth group to come to our lock-in." Huh? Where'd that come from?

"Sure," Connie said. "You're so motivated, you call and ask." My eyes got big, and I let out a nervous giggle. There was no hiding the meaning of that kind of giggle.

Connie looked at me, a funny expression on her face, "Julie, you know David is married, right?"

"Married?" I asked. My heart sank, and I felt a little nauseated. "Crap," I whispered.

Connie nodded.

"Oh man. Crap," I said again. Then, in almost the same breath I said, "So can we invite them anyway?" Married. Pssh. I still wanted to see him. He was cute.

Consensus was yes, we should still invite them.

"You call, Julie," Connie told me.

"Me?" I squeaked.

She nodded at me. I looked around at everyone else, hoping someone would rescue me. No one did.

"Okay," I whispered, scared but determined. I was going to have to talk to him sometime. Might as well be right then.

Wow, was I nervous. While I dialed the phone (literally dialed – it was an old black rotary phone), my hands shook, and I feared I might throw up everywhere. David answered right away, not giving me the chance to think too much about what I wanted to say.

"David, this is Julie, from the Holbert CYF. We want to know if you and your youth group want to come for a lock-in with us. Our leader, Connie, told me I could call you and ask." I ran it all together without a breath, knowing he wouldn't remember any of us, much less me.

He laughed, a deep laugh. A cute laugh, if cute could be used to describe a laugh, that is. I liked his laugh. "Well, Julie from the Holbert CYF, you just tell Connie that we'd be happy to come to Holbert and be locked in a room all night with you Holbert youth." His voice was deep, too. And kind. He sounded just like I thought he would.

I hung up the phone, ran to the bathroom, and locked myself in a stall. Having anyone see me shake all over would be much too embarrassing.

The door to the bathroom opened. "Julie?" Brenda called out to me. She'd come to check on me.

"I'm in here," I yelled from my stall.

"Everything okay? Are they coming?"

"Yeah, he's coming. They're coming." I stepped out of the stall.

She looked at me and made a face. "Aren't you going to flush?"

I laughed. "I didn't go. I was just...I was just hiding."

Brenda shook her head at me. She knew me too well. "He's married, Julie."

"Yeah," I whispered and looked down at my feet. I gathered a big breath and let it out. Confidence and nonchalance. I could pretend that. No one need know that I still thought David cute. I looked back up, raised my eyebrows, and smiled wide. "No biggie," I told her. "It'll just be fun to have the other group here." Liar. I didn't care about the rest of the group.

Brenda smiled back at me. "Good. Let's go back and eat all the cookies."

Sounded good to me.

***

Guess what. I talked to David! Lots. Even with close to 30 people there, somehow he and I ended up spending most of the time together. It started with basketball. How could I pass up a challenge?

"Hey, Julie." I looked up, and he threw the ball at me in a line drive. Without breaking the conversation I was having with Brenda, I snatched the ball out of the air and chucked it right back.

He caught it and laughed, surprised. "Wow, impressive. Let's see that on the court."

"Oh, Brother, you'd better watch out then." I was pretty thrilled by the whole thing, and the thought of playing ball kept my nerves at bay. I wasn't a high school basketball player, but I could hold my own on the court.

He held the ball above his head. His height didn't concern me.

"Hey!" I yelled, and when he looked down at me, I leapt up and grabbed the ball out of his hands. I dribbled around him and shot the ball. Score!

I rebounded my own basket and hugged the ball to my chest.

"Beat that!" I grinned at him.

He laughed. His smile filled his face. I stood frozen for a second. That smile threw me off.

"How'd you do that? You're so little." He was still grinning.

"Little but mighty." I laughed back at him and stuck my right arm out, flexing my bicep.

He shook his head and snatched the ball back out of my hand. Before I could move, he shot up and over my head.

"Tie game, Julie." He bent down to tie his shoe. "Time to get serious now."

We played for at least an hour, mostly just the two of us but occasionally with another kid or two stepping in. He won, but barely.

"Good try, kiddo." He patted me on top of my head.

I ducked and laughed at him. "Pssh, I let you win."

"Think what you must." He was laughing, too.

After ball, it seemed easy to hang out together. We played pool, watched movies, and talked into the night.

Somehow in all our conversations during that lock-in he discovered my deep and abiding love for the Rolling Stones, most specifically, Mick Jagger. David could perfectly mimic just about everyone, including Mick, who was the first of many I heard him impersonate.

David teased me mercilessly all night long. None of us slept much. It's too hard to sleep on pool tables and hard tiled floors, so the next morning we stumbled down to the fellowship hall grumbling about the early hour. Sleepy as I was, I tried to time my arrival to just after David's so I could sit by him. It had to look casual, of course. No need to give away my plan.

I stepped into the dining hall not far behind him, watching him closely. Instead of sitting, he headed over to talk to a couple of the guys from his group. I stood there unsure what to do.

"Julie!" I heard Brenda call and looked her way to see her beckoning me. She'd saved me a seat. Shoot. I had to go. Otherwise, everyone would notice and wonder. I forced a smile and headed that way.

"Thanks for saving me a seat," I called out to her, my voice too shrill. My goal was to show how happy and excited I was to be there and how unaffected I was by the fact that David was in the room. I wouldn't look at him, I decided.

That plan might have worked had he not sat directly across from me. Every time I glanced up from my sausage and toast, there he was.

"Hey, Julie. Hey, Julie." His whisper wasn't really a whisper. He might as well have been yelling. Everybody looked at me. I was so embarrassed but pretended he didn't phase me.

I lifted my head to see what he wanted, trying to act like it was no big deal. Immediately, he grinned at me and then stuck his lips out teasing me again about Mick. I made a face at him and turned my head. I could hear him laughing at me.

"Hey, Julie. Hey, Julie." And so it went. I looked and he'd make some crazy face or say something ridiculous. It wasn't long before I could no longer pretend to be annoyed. He was too funny, and he had me laughing despite my attempts at acting cool. Soon, everyone jumped in and started talking to David and over us. Chaos but fun. For those few minutes before, though, it had just been us.

Mid-Winter Retreat Part 2 - The Next Year

A year passed - a year full of school, hanging out with friends, playing tennis, first dates (and second). I dated Daniel. And then Drew. And somewhere in there I dated Brian, too. I remember talking to friends about their boyfriends and listening to them go on and on about how 'in loooove' they were. I wasn't in love. Not that I didn't want to be. I just - wasn't. I felt on hold. I mean, I lived my life but it mostly seemed as if I was living it from the outside, going through the motions. You know, just doing what it was I was supposed to do. I stayed out of my house as much as possible. When I had to be home, I typically holed myself up in my bedroom. What a relief it was when January rolled around and it was time for our Mid-Winter retreat again. None of us knew who exactly would be at the retreat, but I prayed and prayed David would be there. Unfortunately, on Friday night, there was no sign of him.

The next morning in the mess hall, Brenda and I worked to prepare breakfast for the entire camp. The preparation of each meal fell to a different youth group. The rest of our youth had stayed in bed. Brenda and I didn't want to be awake at 6:00 a.m. either, but breakfast had to be made.

Because it was so early, no one had been in to build a fire in the fireplace, and the cold was almost unbearable. With each egg I cracked, my fingers got colder and colder until I could barely pick the next one up.

"Hello, look at me," Brenda said in a silly voice. I glanced up and saw her with a piece of bacon pressed across her mouth, shaped in a Joker-like smiley face. What a goof.

I burst out laughing as she pranced around singing a silly song, still holding the bacon to her mouth. We carried on so loudly, we didn't hear the squeeeak, slam of the screen door announcing a new arrival to the mess hall.

"Are you girls having fun?" A deep voice interrupted our goofiness. I looked at the kitchen door and saw a tall, trim, bearded man wearing faded blue jeans and a red knit shirt. I didn't recognize him at first, and then he smiled. I knew that smile.

"Do you remember me?" he asked.

"David!"

He stepped over to me and gave me a quick hug. David was there! I'd been so afraid I wouldn't see him again.

"You're here!" I think I squeaked when I said it. Brenda looked at me funny. I didn't care, though.

"Ohhh, we drove early this morning," he told us. "A few of the kids had a basketball game last night they couldn't miss, but we didn't want to miss the retreat either."

I smiled. "I'm glad you're here." Brenda looked at me again, surprised. I had surprised myself, too. Timidity typically held me back from making such admissions.

He patted me on the back. "Me, too, Juliebean. Me too."

This time we heard the door squeak open and slam shut as he left. I just stood there grinning. Juliebean. I thought that was about the best thing I'd ever heard. All of a sudden, I realized what I'd been on hold for all these past months. David. It didn't make any sense, really. I didn't understand what exactly that meant. Logically, it was stupid. I knew that. Illogically, well, what can I say? I'd never felt quite so happy as I did when David was there. Already.

The rest of the weekend blurred by. Keynotes, small groups, long hikes in woods overlooking the lake, prayer and quiet time filled the days. Games and a dance interspersed our faith lessons. Being together like that every minute of the day, we couldn't help but form strong bonds.

The First Letter

"You have a letter." Mom called out to me from the kitchen as I came in. "It's from a bank." I could hear the question in her voice, but I didn't have any idea why a bank would send me a letter either.

I unfolded the letter carefully glancing quickly over it. My heart thumped when I saw the signature. David. I'd forgotten he only worked as youth director part time. He also worked at a bank. We'd talked about it the Saturday afternoon at the retreat, that he hoped to someday be able to do youth ministry or some kind of service work full time.

"Who's it from?" Mom asked.

"David. From camp." My voice was quiet.

I read slowly to myself:

Julie,

It sure was good to see you again last weekend! The Lord has really given you a winning personality. Always a smile and a kind word for everyone…

Love in Him,
David

Oh. He wrote about Jesus. I hoped it would be more personal…about me. Never mind that David was married. I tried to ignore that fact. But he said I had a winning personality. He thought I was kind. I wasn't convinced it was true. Even so, I never realized being kind was something to be recognized for. I liked it, though. I never knew what people thought of me, and I worried about it. That little misfit girl I used to be still took over sometimes. I hadn't yet figured out who I was, but I knew I wouldn't mind being the person David described. My hands shook. I had so much to process, so much to figure out. Such a deep and important message. I needed to think about it a while. I still felt a little bummed it wasn't more about me, though, you know.

"What's it say?" Mom asked.

Carefully I folded the letter up and slipped it back into the envelope. Holding it close to my chest, I quickly headed toward the stairs. "Just a hi from camp. Nothing really." I knew Mom wanted more, but it was for me. My letter. Words that made me feel…good and important and cared about. I couldn't let that be taken away from me, and she would, I knew. Somehow she would criticize and call it stupid. It might be words or a snotty gasp and roll of her eyes. She'd been doing it to me as long as I could remember. For one of the only times in my life, I defied my mother directly and kept walking out of the room, clutching my letter and ignoring her questioning stare.

He's Still – Summer Church Camp

I stepped through the door soundlessly, having left my flip flops scattered on the sidewalk out front. A group of us had been playing horseshoes for the last hour and a half and the hot sand felt good between my toes, so I stayed barefoot even though Wayne, the camp director, told us repeatedly of the dangers of running barefoot through the country grass.

Sweating and incredibly thirsty, I ran inside to grab a glass of ice water thinking no one would be there during our camp activity time. People spread out in all directions outside with various activities. No one should have been indoors. Without looking, I darted through the door into the great room to head across to the kitchen. Out of the corner of my eye, I saw something. Someone. And I stopped fast. It was so quiet in there. I could only hear the tick tick of the refrigerator. Why would anyone be inside in the quiet? I looked to the corner and saw David sitting in the center of the brown leather couch, his head bowed. I wasn't sure if he was praying or sleeping. He hadn't heard me come in; my shoeless feet made no noise on the tile floor.

I stood there stuck, not knowing if I should continue on to the kitchen and run the risk of disturbing him or if I should back out of the room. I'd never seen him without a mob of people around him. He always held center stage in a room. I looked away, trying to decide what to do. Too curious not to, I looked back. His tan shorts had pulled up a little above his knees as he sat, and I couldn't help but notice his legs. Good legs. Strong legs covered with plenty of curly brown hair. I couldn't help but wonder what it would be like to touch his leg right there where the edge of his shorts ended. He wore the blue camp t-shirt we all had. With his head bowed, the back of his hair didn't quite touch the top of his collar like usual.

I decided to back slowly out of the room. Whether he slept or prayed, it was obviously a private time. I stepped backwards, still watching David. I don't know whether I made a sound or if he caught the movement out of the corner of his eye or what, but slowly he looked up. Freezing in place, I wondered briefly if I should just turn and run.

I'm sure I looked like a deer caught in the headlights. He made me so nervous. When he saw me, though, he smiled, a big slow lazy smile that reached his eyes and warmed me despite the fact it made me even more nervous. If that makes any sense at all.

"Hi, Julie." Quiet. Soft. Not the voice I was used to hearing entertain and motivate. Again, I felt warmth spread through me. What was that?

"Hi, David." I whispered back at him and then spoke a little louder. "I'm sorry. I didn't mean to bother you."

He smiled again, bigger this time although I wouldn't have believed that possible. Patting the couch next to him, he said, "You should always bother me. Come here."

I stepped closer, scared about the small space I would have to fit in between him and the edge of the couch, but he scooted over and made more room so that when I did sit, we didn't come close to touching. Disappointing but not. Such confusing feelings.

"It's so quiet," I continued to whisper, not wanting to disturb the stillness. "I'm not used to you being so…" I trailed off, realizing that probably wasn't the nicest thing to say that I thought he was loud.

David laughed then and gently swatted my leg with the back of his hand. Playful. "I can be quiet, Julie."

"Mm hmm," I nodded but squinted my eyes towards him, teasing him, and he laughed again. I'd only recently begun to tease him back. I liked his response when I did. He would laugh, sometimes a low, deep chuckle and sometimes right out loud, a big, full laugh that filled the space around him and reached out in every direction. No matter which laugh, he always smiled in a way that filled his entire face. I loved being the one to make him smile like that.

"Everyone needs down time, right? Even me."

"Were you sleeping?"

"No, just thinking. Praying a little. Being still," he answered me, tugging his shorts back down towards his knee, more like a nervous habit, though, and not really out of necessity. They weren't riding up too high. I'm not sure why 'nervous' came to mind. I couldn't imagine David being nervous like I always was, but that's how it seemed. I thought back to my previous idea about touching his leg and looked away, embarrassed. As if he could read my mind. Goodness, I hoped he couldn't ever read my mind.

"How do you spend your down time, Julie?"

"I don't know." I hadn't really thought about it. "Laying on my bed. Listening to music. That kind of thing."

"Do you talk to God?"

I thought about that. I guess sometimes I did. Especially when I wanted something. Oh, I don't just mean material things. Just anything, happiness, help on a test remembering information. That kind of thing. "I talk to Him some, I guess." I said.

David shifted positions so that he was turned, facing me. I could feel him staring at me, and I was afraid to look at him. Afraid to meet his gaze.

"Do you listen, too?" He asked me.

"What?" I took a chance and glanced at him, hoping he wouldn't see me looking. He did. Oops. Dark blue eyes staring at me, searching my face, watching me. He could see inside me. Well, crap. He really could read my mind. With that gaze, how could he not? No one had ever looked at me like that before. I glanced away and played with my ring, the one Dad gave me for my 18th birthday.

"Do you listen to God?" He asked again.

I shrugged. "I don't know. I've never thought about it." I dared to glance back at him. He still stared. So intense. I didn't look away, though. Not this time.

He grinned just a little half grin. "Try it. You'll be amazed at what He'll tell you."

Very slowly, I nodded. He didn't say anything else. He just kept looking. Staring. I kept that eye contact too as long as I could and then…

"I'm going to go," I went back to a whisper. My voice didn't seem to want to work. I couldn't get the words to come out any louder.

He nodded and touched my shoulder briefly. "I'm glad you bothered me, Julie."

"Psshh," I hit his arm playfully. Jumping up, I turned and ran back across the room, out the door, forgetting all about the glass of water I'd so desperately wanted not ten minutes before. He did that to me. Jumbled my brain so I couldn't think straight.

David wanted me to think so hard. I just wasn't that deep. I couldn't think about the things he wanted me to. I didn't really want to, did I? I wanted fun and games and guys. God was there, sure. Wasn't He always there? I didn't want to listen to Him. What if He asked me to do something I didn't want to do?

All that was fine for David, but it didn't really relate to me. I simply wasn't interested. I wasn't deep enough. It was great he was. And he was cute, too. So cute. That's all that mattered to me.

Broken Pitcher

Carefully, I stirred the iced tea and lifted the overfull pitcher hoping to make it to the fridge without spilling any.

Just almost there, I felt it slipping. Before I could stop it, it dropped through my hands and hit the floor with a bang. Tea flew everywhere and the pitcher crackkkked and shattered.

"Oh my God!" I heard my mother yell. I didn't realize she had come in the side door. "My pitcher! What a mess!"

I looked at her and for a moment I wanted to curl inside myself…or I wanted to run and get away from her. Instead, I closed my eyes briefly and whispered a silent prayer, please Lord. I felt a peace come over me. Strength but not anger. David had taught me about that in the short time I had known him; I could count on the Lord for strength and peace. I listened to everything David told me, mostly to hear his voice and to have an excuse to look at him while he talked. Who knew, though. Maybe it would work. I thought I'd give it a try.

"Mom," I said, and my calm but strong tone of voice surprised even me. "It's okay. It's a pitcher. I'll clean it up, and I'll replace the pitcher."

"Oh..oh…" she sputtered, probably surprised I had spoken up to her. "No, you don't have to do that." She was still abrupt, but she backpedaled her criticism quickly.

"But I will," I responded.

And I did. I cleaned up the tea, drove to the store, and returned to present a new pitcher to my mother.

"You didn't have to do that." She sounded bewildered.

Truthfully, it stunned me, too. Where the heck had my confidence come from? I'd accidentally broken the pitcher, and nothing catastrophic happened. I wasn't 'bad' because of it. I remembered a time when I'd bumped into the dining table and broken a plate. By the time Mom finished berating me for it, I was convinced

I was a horrible kid. Now, I knew better. Accidents happen to everyone. I was a good person, not bad at all. David told me so. Knowing David believed in me filled me with a confidence unfamiliar to me. Still in its infancy, I struggled to remember it was there which caused my first reaction to still be fear. When I remembered, though, and when I remembered to lean on God, too, it was okay. I could handle anything.

The Types of Love

David and I stood in the parking lot of the restaurant, both of us leaning against the church bus he had driven to pick me up, facing each other, deep in conversation. Time passed so quickly, and I'd finished my first year of college. We kept in touch throughout the year through letters. Every Wednesday, I raced to the mailboxes in the dorm lobby because David seldom missed putting a letter in the mail to me on Monday or Tuesday. I'd hold that letter to my chest and make myself wait until I was back in my room to open it. Now, in the beginning of my sophomore year, he'd begun coming to see me. We'd been out to eat together several times, our friendship growing as we sat talking together at various restaurant tables, sometimes for hours. This time had been no different. When we finally made it out of the restaurant, we continued our conversation outside. Reaching into my purse, I pulled out a picture and held it out to him, a picture of another David, the one who worked at the front desk in my dorm.

"I'm gonna marry this guy," I announced. It was true, I had decided. I could easily picture a life with this other David. Cute, friendly, conveniently located in the lobby of my dorm. No matter that he wasn't really interested in me, I could still imagine it. In my imagination, I could control the situation and make it what I wanted. I did that, had always done that. When I stayed in control, nothing hurt me. I could easily block myself off from anything that made me feel too much. That way, I couldn't be disappointed.

Still, even though I could imagine it, I really was kidding…at least some. I waited to see this David's reaction.

David reached for the picture, brow furrowed. "What? Why?" he asked me.

"Because he's just so cute!"

"No." He shook his head emphatically. "No, Julie. You can't marry someone just because he's cute."

"I don't know why not," I answered. "Besides, he's really nice, too."

"Do you love him?"

I grinned at him. He didn't realize I was kidding. "I love that he's cute!" I looked up at the sky, at a passing car, anywhere but directly at David.

He reached out and touched my shoulder. "Juliebean," he started, glanced away from me as if he were trying to decide what to say and then looked back at me, his gaze intense. "Julie, listen. Love." He let that word die off on a sigh of breath. Started again…"Do you know about love…the types of love?"

I didn't even really know what love was. I loved pizza. I loved the guys I'd had crushes on, but I knew it wasn't real love. I knew I loved my dad, my brother, my sister. But what did that mean when we were talking about loving a man (boy, whatever). I had no answer. Slightly, I shook my head. No.

David leaned against the church van. Gesturing to emphasize his point, he continued. "There are three main types of love; well, I think there are four, but these three are the ones most important, okay? - philos, eros, and agape."

"Okay," I could follow him so far.

"Philos is compassionate love, the kind you'd feel for a friend."

"Like Brenda."

"Sure, or anyone. Even just mankind. Brotherly love."

"Okay," I said.

He continued. "Eros is romantic love – that probably speaks for itself, doesn't it?"

I nodded. I listened. The sound of his voice kept my attention as always. His words, whether they were silly, entertaining, or serious, impacted me …always.

"Eros is what you might feel for a movie star…or a cute boy. Or most importantly, when you fall in love with someone, right?"

"Right," I responded automatically.

"And then there's agape, the most important of all. Spiritual love. The kind of love Christ has for us. The kind of love He wants us to have for everyone else."

I nodded as if I understood completely. His eyes were so blue. I stared at him thinking about his blue eyes and hoping that I looked as if I were intent…and wise.

"Julie, it's common to have one or two of these types of love for people. That's typically what happens. It's rare to have all three types of love for one person.

That's what you want, though, when you're deciding who to marry. You want to find the person you feel all three types of love for."

I nodded at him, listening but not. I loved him; I knew that. At least in the philos and eros way. I didn't quite get the other. Christ's love? Sure, okay. It didn't matter, anyway. David would never love me in those ways. He'd never given me any indication that he would. I knew that. It was okay, though. As long as I could keep seeing him, I didn't care. I had no idea why he was telling me all this about love. I couldn't really marry this other guy, anyway, and I sure didn't love him. He only ever treated me like a cute little sister. I always did stuff like that, imagine the situation and control it. That's what worked for me, or at least kept me from getting too close and getting hurt. It kept people at a distance, and that suited me just fine. I think I just wanted to see what David would say.

"Okay, David." We stood quietly. He was staring at me, I could tell, but I couldn't look up at him. It felt too serious. Too…something. I stepped past him carefully making sure I didn't brush up against him and climbed the van steps taking my place in the front row seat right behind the driver's seat.

"Thanks for lunch."

Three days later

I stepped out to get the mail and found a package. The return address – David. Trying to draw out the suspense, I made myself look through all the other mail first when I got to the kitchen table with it. I saved

David's package for last. From the feel of it, I could tell it was a book.

Slowly, I slid my finger under the flap of the tan envelope and pulled out the book...*The Four Loves* by C.S. Lewis. Tucked inside the front cover was a small white piece of paper on which David had written, "Read this. Love in Him, David".

That's all he wrote. Despite knowing better, I still held out hope that he would declare his undying love, and he kept writing about God and spiritual things. Ugh.

Mission Work and Jelly Beans

Even while away at college, I kept in close contact with the group of kids from my church who I had grown up with. When Connie, my old youth director, invited us to get back together so that we could travel to downtown Oklahoma City for mission work, I immediately agreed. Just before I left, David visited me and slipped me a tiny wrapped package.

"Put this in your bag. Don't open it until after your first day," he told me.

It was all I could do not to open it right away when he left, but I didn't. I packed it carefully with the rest of my things and saved it as he had asked.

Our first day, we worked in a dilapidated church, hauling out junk, cleaning, preparing to paint the next day. By the end of the day, we were exhausted and wanted nothing more than to sleep. My childhood friend, Brenda, went with us and we set up our sleeping bags in the corner of the fellowship hall next to each other so we could talk and catch up with each other's lives. I hadn't seen her for at least a year.

I pulled out David's gift. "What's that?" Brenda asked.

I shrugged trying to act casual. "It's from David." I didn't want to open it in front of anyone, but I had no choice. Carefully, I unwrapped the red and white striped paper and pulled open the top flap of a little cardboard box. A folded note sat on top. I moved it aside and found a bag. Of jellybeans. Laughing, I shook my head. I didn't understand why he'd sent jellybeans.

Turning away from her just a little to give myself as much privacy as possible, I read the note:

These made me think of you. Hope they add some sweetness to the end of a day of hard work. You are making a difference. I'm praying for you. David

No one had ever given me anything so sweet. Nor had anyone ever told me he was praying for me. Not where I believed they really meant it. "I'm praying for you" always just seemed to be something people said but didn't necessarily follow through with. Oh, I know that must sound skewed or bitter, but I believed it. I'd been guilty of it myself, saying I was praying for someone and then not. I always said it sincerely at that moment but later, I'd forget.

David meant it, though. I knew he did. He cared. About me. He thought I could make a difference. I wanted to, but how? If only I could be the way he seemed to see me. I kept trying, but it never seemed enough.

"What's it say?" Brenda interrupted my thoughts.

Discreetly, I wiped away the tears forming at the corner of my eye and put on my fake smile happy face. "He's praying for us." I told her, not wanting to share his words exactly. David's letters were mine, only for me. He was my own secret world where someone actually cared about me. Really cared. Deeply. I didn't know how it could be real, but it was. Either that or I was just fooling myself again. Still. Something.

"Oh, that's nice," she fluffed up her pillow and lay down. "I'm sleepy. But not too sleepy for jelly beans. Hint Hint." She laughed.

I slipped the note into the zippered side pocket of my backpack and tossed her the jellybeans.

We ate them all in about two minutes.

Hey Jules

"Come with me, Juliebean."

While I no longer attended Mid-Winter retreat as a camper, David invited me each year as a counselor. I had just stepped out of the mess hall and started down the ramp when I heard David call. I glanced up and saw him across the sidewalk.

In one hand, he clutched his guitar by the neck, with the other he kind of flopped his hand up in a wave to me. I waved back and stood for a second. It took me that second to find the courage I needed to actually approach him even though he had called to me instead of the other way around. Once I found that courage, which I did quickly, I hurried toward him.

"What are we doing?"

"Just follow me."

Okay. I didn't ask anything else. I just went. We stepped to the edge of the woods, and from there, I could see the lake through the trees. To get down to the shore from where we stood, we'd have to skirt the woods to take a path or barrel through and try to make our way down the steep incline, through the trees. Knowing David by then, I imagined we would barrel through.

We stood quietly. I didn't know what he was thinking and felt too shy to ask him. All of a sudden we heard feet. Lots of them.

"Hey, where are you going?" Voices shouted at us. I looked around and saw three or four campers coming our way. A sinking feeling came over me when I realized they were going to join us. I knew David would never turn anyone away. I really wouldn't either even if I wanted to. Sure enough, he answered them right away.

"We're heading down to the lake." I heard something in his voice. Something slight that I don't think they would have heard. Hesitation? Maybe. I looked over at him, curious. He caught my eye, gave me a little grin, and winked at me. I knew then he wasn't thrilled about the others either. I wasn't quite sure what that meant, but I liked it.

The other kids crowded around, several of them asking at once can we come, can we come.

"Sure, sure," David said to them. "Come with us. We're heading down through those trees. Be careful because it's steep." Just as I thought, we wouldn't be looking for a path but plowing through the middle of the woods instead.

The kids barreled down in front of us. David held back a little, and I stayed next to him.

He picked his way carefully through the trees, trying to keep his guitar from the branches hanging low. I stepped through the rocks and brushed past the branches.

"Wait a second." David shuffled down the hill a little further. He stopped and turned around, slinging the guitar over his shoulder.

I looked at his outstretched hand. Slowly I reached for it. His fingers tightened around mine as he helped me down the rocky incline. Immediately, my hand started sweating despite the fact the temperature hovered around 40. How embarrassing. I wondered if I could discreetly let go, wipe my hand off, and grab hold again. Probably not. Besides, I didn't want to let go. I'd have to deal with the embarrassment. It was worth the risk. I was such a mess.

"Oh, sorry." I caught myself as I tripped over a rock and almost plowed into him. He laughed, gripped my hand tighter, and tried to reach up and around me with his other arm to hold me steady but ended up whapping me in the side with the guitar. We both giggled; I glanced quickly up to see his face. He was staring straight down at me, and I caught his eyes directly. Why did he stare at me like that? No one ever did that.

"Oh." I was flustered for a minute, and I looked away as fast as I could.

"Let's go on, Julie." I could hear amusement in his voice. Ugh. I hated that 'amused' voice. Not that I didn't want to amuse him, but…ugh.

I felt him start back down. Without looking but still gripping his hand in mine, I followed. Until we came to a little clearing and he stopped, I spent the time holding onto him and staring at his back. I didn't trust myself to say anything. It would either come out too shaky or too stupid. I was determined not to look any more stupid than I already had. Cool Julie. That's who I was going to be.

The campers who invited themselves along had stopped in the clearing and were waiting for us. Boulders almost perfectly circled the area with trees behind them. We were about halfway down from the camp area to the lake. It looked beautiful, but the wind there close to the water made the air bite.

David hoisted himself and his guitar up onto one of the highest rocks. The others gathered around him. I hung back a little bit and just watched him. They all were talking at him, laughing and making jokes with him. I feared that I'd make a fool of myself, again. So I stayed back and waited.

He played a few songs and some of the kids sang along. I still just watched. I don't remember what he sang then. I remember watching his face, his smile. Listening to his voice. Wishing I was sure enough about myself to be right there with the crowd of kids hanging on to his every note.

Then, I heard my name. Well, kind of.

"Hey Jules, don't make it bad. Take a sad song and make it better…."

David had started his own version of The Beatles, "Hey Jude". I didn't know it then, but it was the first of many times he would add me to a song. I grinned, looked up at him, and found him grinning right back at me. Looking straight at me. For a moment, I didn't notice anyone else, just David. David saw me. I mean, he really saw me. He always watched me, listened to me, knew me. And he still wanted to be my friend. No one had ever truly seen me before. No one else ever has since. Not like David did.

The 'na-na-na-na' part started and David got louder and sillier. The other kids sang along as loudly as they could, breaking the mood. I looked away and when I did glance back at him a minute later, he also stared in another direction…again letting the other kids have his attention. Rowdy, goofy, fun.

Tournament Weekend

Nerves made my hands shake and my stomach nauseous. David stood in my living room in my home. He had a softball tournament in Holbert and for some reason, somehow, I had asked my mother if he could stay with us for the weekend rather than have to rent a motel room.

I'd already shown him the room he'd be staying in – the front bedroom, first on the left as you head up the hallway – and he'd put his bags and softball gear away. Now, I stood in front of him, leaning on the floral couch for support, wondering what came next.

"What do you want to do?" I asked him. He didn't have a game until 7:30; it was only 3:00. I also had a tournament that same weekend, a tennis tournament, but my first match wasn't until 10 a.m. Saturday morning.

He smiled at me, "Anything you want."

I shrugged and grinned back at him. "I have no idea."

"Okay then," he said. "Just show me the town."

Great, show him the town. What was there to show in my not too huge town of about 20,000. Not that it was tiny, I know that, but my familiarity with it kept me from coming up with anything that seemed the slightest bit interesting. I lived in a regular old midwestern town full of burger joints, banks, and too many churches to count.

"We could go visit my friend, Lisa…"

Remember Lisa? My long time tomboy/cheerleader friend? She was the first one to see the picture of David playing his guitar on the mantel, the one I took with my little Sony Disc camera the very first time I saw him. Taking him to meet her allowed me to show him off, and I liked that idea.

David nodded, "Sounds great to me. Lead the way."

We took his car and he drove, but I navigated, of course. As we drove up Washington Avenue, I tried to slow him down in time.

"Wait, David, right here, right here." He drove too fast and wasn't prepared to stop quickly, especially when he saw where I pointed.

"What do you mean right here? There's no house here."

"It's here. Turn in here where this store is."

He hit the brakes hard enough for us to pitch forward a little and swung sharply into the parking lot where I pointed. "But, Julie," he argued, laughing, "This is a liquor store!"

"I know! She lives above it in that little apartment. See those windows? And that little window unit a/c?"

He pulled to a stop and craned his neck looking behind him at the building. "A liquor store? Seriously?"

It was true. Lisa moved out of her parents' home before we graduated high school. They gave her no support at all, and she worked in a little law office for minimum wage; she could barely afford to eat. Even now, two years after graduation, she struggled to make ends meet. I told David that and also about the time she showed up at my parents' house with a can of chili asking to borrow a can opener because it was all she had to eat, and she couldn't get it open.

"Wow," he said. "And she's doing okay?"

"Yeah, she's okay, I guess."

"Have you invited her to church?" he asked me. Of course David would worry about church.

"She goes to her own church, David. She still goes."

"Okay, that's good. And you're serious she lives above the liquor store?" He laughed. He thought it was so funny.

"Yep, you want a bonus drink?"

He laughed again. "I guess not."

"Your loss," I elbowed him, and he reached around and grabbed my arm. I stopped for a minute and looked up at him. He peered down at me, his eyes bright, a slight grin on his face, but he looked serious, too. Contemplative, anyway. I hadn't really seen that look on his face before and wasn't sure what to say. Instead of saying anything, I flashed him a big grin …big like he usually gave me. He laughed and the serious-look moment ended.

"Let's go meet Lisa," he said, heading toward the liquor store. "Julie, I can quite honestly say I've never met anyone who lived above a liquor store."

"Stick around me, David, and I'll show you things you've never seen."

He laughed again, while I was thinking oh my gosh, did I really say that out loud? I peeked over at him, a little afraid, and he raised his eyebrows at me, amused again. I grabbed his elbow and escorted him the rest of the way, anxious to show him off to my friend.

***

"Do you want to swim?" I asked David. We were back at my house early Saturday afternoon. I didn't play the next round of my tournament until 6:00. He didn't have to be at his next game until 8:30. I went with my boyfriend at the time, Keith, to watch David's softball game Friday night, and David came on his own to watch my match that morning. Keith and I had been dating for several months. He was a nice guy, and I liked him fine, but that was all really. David thought it was all 'cute'. He asked me about it sometimes. Mostly he asked in the same way he did about Carl, an old camp boyfriend, and anyone else – 'Do you really like him? Why do you like him? Are you happy?' It made me a little uncomfortable at first talking about my boyfriends with David but it became commonplace after we had known each other a while. I dated other guys because when would I ever date David? Never. My crush on him was all on me. I loved to be with him, but I knew, really, it would never go further. And so, the times in between seeing David I tried to, you know, actually live my own life. I did okay, but in reality, I spent most of the time waiting to see David again and comparing the guys I dated to him. Now, with him right there with me, just the two of us at my house alone together, I wasn't quite sure what to do with him. Our pool seemed like a good choice.

He shook his head, though. "No, let's stay in." He walked over to our piano and using his index finger played a fast-forward version of "Mary Had a Little Lamb". "Do you play?" he asked me.

"Lessons for nine years…but no, not really. Just some."

"Nine years. I bet you're better than you think."

"I'm okay."

"Let me play you a song, is that okay?"

"Sure," I said. I didn't know he even played the piano, just a guitar. And I loved that.

"When I'm through, you can play one for me."

I nodded as he sat down on the piano bench and then scooted himself up a little. I stood there unsure what to do at first. The nearest chair had its back to the piano, and I wanted to watch him, so I sat down on the floor cross-legged looking up at him, ready to listen.

"What are you going to play?"

He didn't answer; he just sat there for a few seconds. And then he started … fingers flying over the keyboard… Elton John's "Crocodile Rock". I could not believe how good he was. I had no idea. I was floored. I stared, mouth gaping open.

He sang, "I remember when rock was young. Me and Julie had so much fun …." Wow, his voice! And his playing. What? His fingers flew over the keyboard. Incredible. I had no idea. He went through the whole song changing poor Susie's name to Julie throughout. I sat there stunned, grinning until my face hurt.

And the "Julie went and left us for some foreign guy"… always teasing me. In college, when I'd first dated Philippe, from France, and then the Canadian (I called him the Canadi-man), Darren, David teased me endlessly. He did a perfect French accent, and he kept me in stitches impersonating my foreign boyfriends. I didn't date either of them longer than a couple of months, but David refused to let me forget them.

David turned his head to grin at me and waggled his eyebrows up and down when he sang, "Julie wore her dresses tight". So embarrassing, but I liked it, too. You know? It was just so cheesy but so much fun. He knew it.

He finished "Crocodile Rock" and went straight into "Your Song". "It's a little bit funny, this feeling inside…" and "how wonderful life is while you're in the world."

And then, "If I was a sculptor…" and the laugh. I remember his laugh.

I sat motionless watching his fingers covering the keyboard, his face so expressive, so passionate.

He finished and turned to look at me. I know I still sat there awestruck, staring at him. "Wow!" I said.

And he laughed, "Did you like it?"

"Yes!" Amazing.

He stood up. "It's your turn now."

"Noooo way," I answered. "Not now. Not after that."

"I want to hear you, too."

"No, David. No. I'm just going to savor the sounds that are still in my ears."

He laughed again and sat down beside me on the floor and crossed his legs, too. Our knees touched, and I jerked mine up but then let it ease its way back down until they touched again. He didn't move.

"How long have you been playing?" I asked him.

"Pretty much forever," he grinned. He lifted his knee and bumped mine.

"Yeah, I can tell." I bumped him back.

"You're not going to play for me, huh? So then what now? You pick."

I looked down at my hands and kind of shrugged my shoulders. He leaned over then and bumped my shoulder with his.

"Hey," I bumped him back harder but lost my balance and started to fall over. Laughing, he put his arm around me and steadied me. I could have sat like that forever, but he had other ideas.

He stood up, held his hand out, and helped me up. "Let me take you to get ice cream."

Ice cream? I thought. Like a little kid.

"Okay," I said.

Embracing Life

Besides the yearly retreat, David invited me to chaperone youth group activities, too. For my first stint as chaperone, I traveled to Six Flags amusement park with them. It worked out really well. My still boyfriend, Keith, usually jealous of any other man I talked with, loved David. He drove me to meet up with the church bus and sent me off with the only man he trusted who also happened to be the only guy I thought I might actually love.

That's how I ended up on hot asphalt in Texas in July. I wore short white shorts and a soft white top with spaghetti straps. My tennis tan was in full form which looked great with the white, I knew. However, my white, white feet threw off the tan's perfection. My flip-flops didn't come close to covering them up like my tennis shoes did. That was the disadvantage of being on a tennis court hours each day and having crew socks be the style.

"Shame you can't play in flip flops, right Juliebean?" David had teased me earlier. So funny.

He finished giving the rules and riot act and meeting times and places and all that to his kids. They had to stay in at least pairs but could otherwise go out on their 'own'. They agreed to meet back in two hours, and off they went.

David stepped back to me. "Looks like it's you and me, baaayby!" I looked away. He still made me nervous. "Yep," I said, hoping that sounded somewhat intelligent but knowing that it really didn't.

"What do you want to do first?"

People passed us right and left, couples, families, all heading to rides and games and junk food. I loved Six Flags and rode pretty much everything. None of the rides bothered me much except one – the Spinnaker. I had never ridden the Spinnaker and planned never to. It looked almost like a closed in Ferris Wheel but it lay flat on its side. Riders had to get into the car and straddle a bench, one right behind the other. They closed a lid which, I heard, had a strong magnet holding it in place. I don't know if that was true or not, but if it was, it didn't sound strong enough to me. Then, the ride went 'round and 'round like a merry-go-round, faster and faster until it started lifting up. It continued its lift until it hung straight up and down, and it flew in circles. It did not look fun to me at all. I made the mistake of saying that to David.

He grinned at me, mischievous David, oh I should have stayed quiet about it. "Julie. If that's the one you're scared of, that's the one we have to ride first."

"No, David. I can't. I mean it."

"You don't mean it. You'll love it." He faced me, putting his hands on my bare shoulders.

"No way."

"Come on." And before I could say another word, he swung around and pulled me by the arm toward the one ride I never wanted to get on.

"No…." it was a half-hearted attempt at 'no'. If David wanted to ride the Spinnaker, we were going to ride the Spinnaker. I gave in quickly. What else could I do? David said I had to.

Of course, that didn't mean I wasn't a little scared. I went along, though. I really do think I would have gone anywhere with him.

We waited in a line that seemed to go way too fast. Weren't amusement park ride lines supposed to take forever? This one didn't. Too soon, it was our turn.

David held the door to an open car steady for me while I climbed in, self-conscious about stepping up and into a rocking car, first of all afraid my rear would stick out and look totally huge (what a girl thing to worry about), and second, afraid I would trip over myself. Fortunately, I made it up and in.

"Whoaaaa," I had to grab the sides to keep steady. A long black padded bench ran up the middle. I threw one leg over to straddle it and hoped there was nothing on the seat that would stain my white shorts. Eww.

"Ack," I shrieked as the car tilted to the side. David climbed up but with no one to hold it, it rocked wildly. "Scoot up, Juliebean," he told me. I moved forward in the seat and he threw his leg over the bench and settled in behind me. I pressed myself as far up at the front of the bench as I could. All of a sudden, it occurred to me that we were the only two in that car. Our very close proximity scared me to death. It didn't seem to bother him. Nothing ever did. At least, that's what I thought then.

The rocking of the car slowed down a little, but I still held on to the side rails. The worker came around to check to make sure our lid closed securely.

"I changed my mind," I told David.

He laughed. "Too late."

I gripped the rails tighter.

"You know, Julie, you might as well scoot back here now," he said.

"Oh? Why?"

"I think it would be better than you slamming back here against me once the ride starts."

He made a good point. It probably did make sense for me to slide back against him since surely the force of the ride would send me back that way anyway. Much better that I not fly into him and smash him.

"Okay," I said, but I didn't move.

I jumped when I felt his hands on my waist. "Slide back here," he said again.

He pulled me back into the V of his legs, and I could feel his chest against my back. Oh. My. Again, he seemed oblivious. I, however, felt my heart thumping wildly, and I thought I might pass out.

The ride started moving. Slowly. David put his arms further around my waist to hold me in place. I sat up very straight. The grinding of the gears got louder and louder. I could feel his mouth next to my ear, and he whispered, "Do you scream when you ride a roller coaster, Julie?"

"No way," I answered him. Of course I didn't scream. How embarrassing would that be? People would stare.

"You don't?"

I shook my head.

He still whispered, mouth right next to my ear, sending goosebumps shivering up my arms, "Oh, Julie. You have to. To truly experience a roller coaster ride, you have to scream. It's the only way. Embrace it. Feel it. Live it."

"Mmm, I don't think so."

The Spinnaker flew faster and faster. I shifted from side to side trying to grip tight to the side rails still as David wrapped his arms tighter around me.

"Do it, Julie. Experience the ride. Do it for me."

"I don't think so, David." I shook my head again.

All of a sudden, the car shifted position as the center beam of the entire ride begin to lift. Once we started up like that, I slid back tight against him. He locked his arms and held me to him. Faster and faster we soared.

The exhilaration thrilled me. Without warning and definitely unintentionally, I let out a little yell. David laughed, and I yelled again. It really did make a difference. What a blast!

David shouted out too and soon we both began screaming our heads off, laughing hysterically as we slammed from side to side.

The ride began lowering and the speed slightly dropped. We stopped screaming but couldn't stop laughing.

"What did I tell you?" David had his mouth close to my ear. It tickled. My arms broke out in goosebumps again; I hoped he wouldn't notice.

"You were right. That was a blast," I agreed.

"That's how you need to embrace life, Julie. Go all out. Feel it all. Live it."

I just nodded and grinned.

When we slowed down enough, David pulled his arms from around me, and I scooted forward just a little so that I wasn't still pressed into his lap. I didn't want to, but it was awkward otherwise.

He helped me down out of the car and then dropped my hand. The moment was over, but I knew I would never forget it.

Let's Dance

Music blared. Harold stood by the screen door making sure no teenagers snuck out of the dance to disappear into the night to make out. He'd caught me out there once a few years before. With Carl. From David's youth group. To me, Carl was just a camp boyfriend. I guess he liked me more than that because he told David all about me. David asked me about it once, and I just shrugged. "He was a nice guy," I told him. Carl was fine, cool even, and pretty cute, but after camp when it was all said and done, well, he was just a camp boyfriend. He wrote me a letter, but I didn't write him back.

For the third year in a row, I counseled Mid-Winter retreat. Counseling probably didn't exactly describe my role. I really didn't do anything helpful with the kids. David wanted me to go, so I did. This particular year, I'd talked my sister, Megan, into going, too, and now, she and I sat over against the windows watching the kids dance. Well, I think Megan was watching the kids. I couldn't stop looking at David. As usual, he was the center of attention. He danced with this girl and that girl. A song would end and another girl would be right there asking him to dance with her. I just watched, a little jealous but not willing to ask him. He was such the gentleman, keeping an appropriate distance but always talking and smiling with each of the girls. At 20, I was quite a few years older than they were, but I still hadn't quite realized that. I felt like a kid.

The song playing ended and the first strains of Journey's "Faithfully" began. David appeared in front of me.

"Aren't you going to ask me to dance, Julie?" he laughed. Sometimes I couldn't tell if he was laughing at me or with me. Even when I wasn't laughing. I didn't think he'd laugh at me, though. Maybe.

I just smiled at him and shrugged. I looked away, kind of nervous, and then peeked back at him. He grinned and held his hand out expecting me to actually grab hold of it. "Come and dance with me."

I let him pull me up and followed him onto the dance floor trying to act smooth and hoping he didn't notice my shaking hands. He put his arms around my waist, and I rested mine up on his shoulders clasping my hands around his neck. He smelled so good, like fresh soap and a tiny, far away mist of cologne. I glanced up wanting to search his face, found him looking down at me, and quickly lowered my eyes. Settling my gaze on his chest, I decided that was best place for me to stare. I couldn't bring myself to look back into his eyes while standing that close to him. Every time I peeked up at him, though, he was still looking at me.

Slowly we moved to the music. We swayed back and forth, and I breathed in the smell of David and sang along to the song in my head, "and loving a music man ain't always what it's supposed to be..."

If that moment had lasted forever, I suppose I would have been perfectly happy. Feeling David hold me like that seemed so intimate, so special. He'd danced with a million girls that night, but they'd all asked him. He was the one who asked me. That was special, wasn't it? I wasn't sure, but I wanted it to be.

The song finished but David didn't hurry to let go. "Thank you for the dance, Juliebean," he whispered to me.

I grinned up at him, still feeling shy. "Sure," I said. "Thank you, too.

He flashed me that big full-on smile he had and then pulled back. "See you later." He winked and was gone. The next girl had already grabbed him and he was dancing again. I watched trying to determine whether he held her any differently than he held me. It seemed they weren't quite as close as he and I had been, but maybe it was just perspective. My imagination maybe. Wishful thinking. Surely he didn't hold me closer. During the dance, he looked somewhere over her head the entire time, never down at her. That was definitely different because I knew he'd looked at me through our dance. So maybe I was special to him. Maybe there was a difference.

Or maybe not.

And why did it even matter anyway? He was still married. That hadn't changed. What was wrong with me?

Back in my cabin that night, I realized that my hands smelled like David. I washed my face and brushed my teeth that night using only my left hand so that my right would continue to smell like him. No kidding. How ridiculous, I know. Apparently, I'd regressed to my 12 year old self. I lay in bed and thought of David, wondering about David. Was I special to him? I hoped for it whether I should hope that or not. I didn't want him to know, though. I wanted to be cool and calm and secure. At least, I tried to come across that way. I smelled my hand again, fluffed my pillow, and finally let myself drift off to sleep.

Mischievous David

We sat at our table for two wrapped up in each other, oblivious to the rest of the restaurant. Bennigans was a casual place – burgers, chicken strips, salads – that kind of thing. David and I both loved it for the variety of food, the casual atmosphere, and because it sat out of the way of our normally traveled areas. As always, without meaning to, we called attention to ourselves with our nonstop talk and frequent laughter. I loved to listen to David talk. I loved his voice, I loved the things he said, I loved the way he included me in what he had to say. I spent much of the time we were together like that giggling and the rest of the time thinking hard about the things he challenged me to come up with – the things he forced me to form and voice my opinions on. "What do you think about that, Julie?" he frequently asked me during our conversations. "What do you think of that?" Then, he listened to what I had to say. He cared about what I had to say.

On this particular day, we must have been louder than usual. I didn't realize it, but all of a sudden, David leaned even closer to me, so close our noses almost touched.

He whispered, "Look at that couple. They keep staring at us."

I looked in the direction he indicated, and sure enough there was an older couple turned from their food and staring at us.

"Ignore them," I whispered back, giggling. David grinned, too.

"We must be loud."

"So shhhh," I told him.

He reached over, laying the palm of his hand on my cheek for a quick moment, smiled, and sat back.

"Politics next," he grinned and picked up his Coke. Instead of taking a drink, he swirled the straw around, and kept looking at me, never breaking eye contact.

I looked down. "I have no opinion on politics."

"Oh, shoot. Don't say that. I know you do."

Think, think…I wanted so badly to come up with something intelligent to say, but I just couldn't. Everything I thought of sounded dumb.

"I don't know, David."

He nodded. "That's okay. I'm just wondering about…" and he mentioned some current controversial political agenda.

"I can't believe that!" I responded. "I never really thought…. I don't know why they don't…."

And before I knew it, I became involved in a political discussion. Me. With my own opinions! Who would have ever thought?! Certainly not me.

After rattling off my thoughts, I suddenly realized what I was saying and sat back. "Oh." I took a deep breath and looked at him wide-eyed.

"You know more than you thought, don't you?" David asked me, smiling.

I grinned. "I guess I do have an opinion."

David didn't say anything. Not about that. He leaned close again and whispered instead, "They're still staring. Don't look."

Rather than swinging my gaze around to see the old couple staring at us, I kept my eyes on David. Without looking away from me, he reached over, felt for the salt and pepper shakers and grabbed them both. He put them up to his eyes like goggles and suddenly swiveled around in his seat doing a gooseneck thing and pointed his condiment goggles at the staring old couple. I burst out laughing. The couple quickly looked away.

"David!" I scolded him, but he just laughed as he put the salt and pepper back.

"I bet they don't stare anymore."

"David."

"What?"

"I can't believe you did that."

"To be honest," he said, "Neither can I… it sure was funny, though."

I laughed. That's how it was with David. Completely unexpected.

Faith on the Tower

"Ohhhhh." David sounded miserable. He sat, pale-faced and slouched back on the bench, hands on his stomach. "I think we rode that Scrambler a few times too many," he groaned.

He did look a little pale. I sat beside him holding in the little huff of impatience that almost escaped. Selfishly, I was disappointed he was sick.

"Are you going to be okay?" I asked him, hoping the answer would be a quick yes.

He gave me a kind of half grin. "I will be," he said. "I'm sorry. I'm old." And then dramatically, he let out another, "Ohhhhh."

I laughed. "No, you're not. You're fine. It's fine."

"Thanks, Julie. I really am sorry." He reached out and touched the back of my hand. I looked quickly over at him, surprised and a little curious, but he jerked his hand back just as quickly and then tried to cover it by standing up abruptly.

"I think I'm okay to try the Tower. I can handle that. Do you want to try the Tower?" he asked.

The Tower. Hmm. 300 feet high, but steady. I thought I could handle that, too. "Sure, David." I stood up beside him.

"It should be tame," he said. I liked the way he said taaaame. Dragging it out. He made me laugh.

Unfortunately, we didn't count on the hundreds of people who had the same idea we did about trying out the Tower. It was packed and hot. I kept glancing at David to make sure he felt okay. He seemed to be holding his own.

I wasn't so sure about me, though. The people drove me nuts. Too many of them milled around. Finally, we made it to the top. We looked over the edge for a second and then turned around leaning back against the outside wall.

"All these people," I complained.

David looked over at me, and I noticed the sweat across his forehead. He didn't really look like he felt much better. "What about them, Julie? That there are so many or what?"

I shifted and looked down at my feet. "Yeah," I kind of mumbled. "Just that there are so many, and they're so…I don't know," I trailed off. I didn't know how to say what I wanted to say without sounding negative. To be honest, I just didn't really like to be around all those people.

"They all have their own story, don't they?" he asked me.

"Huh?" Wow. Brilliant response. Why couldn't I ever come up with something intelligent to say? I wanted depth, but it escaped me.

"Do you ever think about things like that? Just like we have our own stories that bring us where we are, that motivate us, that shape who we are."

Hmm. No, I hadn't ever really thought about that. I shook my head.

"Think about it," he said. "Really." I guess I looked skeptical.

"Okay, David," I told him. "I'll think about it."

"No really, Julie, listen." He turned to face me, his face so expressive, so intense, so into what he wanted to say, what he wanted me to understand. "Each of these people walking by us, each one who got in our way or didn't or saw us or didn't, you get what I mean, each one has his own story. Maybe they got up this morning and fought with their spouse or their parents or maybe they lost a job or are having money troubles. Maybe they're a rare case where they woke up and they have nothing wrong in their lives. We don't know. What we do know, though, is that they each have a story that led them to how they woke up this morning, that led them to the choices they make and are making, that brought them here on this tower with us at this exact time. And each single one of these people is a little reflection of God whether they understand that they are or not. Do you get what I'm saying?"

I looked up at him, quizzically. "Maybe. Yes?" I actually thought I did understand.

He smiled at me and although he took a tiny step back from me, he reached up and lay his hand on my shoulder. His touch distracted me, but I made myself pay attention to his words. It was hard. He continued by asking me, "Julie, who is the light of the world?"

I answered automatically, "Jesus." I knew that. I'd been taught that all my life. I didn't know what it meant deep down, but I knew the answer. Well, I mean, I knew it logically. I didn't know it, know it.

David nodded and continued, "And when each person is a reflection of God, they reflect that light of Christ. That light is in them."

"Okay." I did understand that.

"It's just not everyone recognizes it yet, and so they go on their way not understanding they are a vessel for the greatest love ever. They don't know how to let that light shine."

I grinned. "Like this little light of mine?"

David laughed. "Exactly."

He dropped his arm and stepped back to my side, leaning against the rail and looking out at the view of Dallas. "It's all about faith, Julie." He wasn't looking at me anymore, just talking. I looked out, too, but then I looked back at him again not wanting to miss anything he said or any 'way' he looked. I wanted to take every bit of it in. He continued, "It is by faith and not by works that we are called to eternal life, Julie. We have to have that faith. We have to know who Christ is and know that we are that reflection of Him."

Faith, not works. I'd heard that, of course, but I wasn't entirely sure about it. I could see both sides, I thought. Meh, it didn't really affect me anyway, so I didn't need to think too much about it. It was a nice thought either way – have the faith or do the works. It was fine either way.

I looked up at David thinking I'd try to come up with something profound to say about it all but instead was a little concerned by the new expression on his face. And by his coloring. He looked grayish. "Are you okay?" I asked him.

He turned to me and tried to grin. "I guess I didn't realize the tower would sway so much up here. I don't think it was good idea to come up here after all."

I laughed and then covered my mouth, "Sorry." I couldn't stop grinning, though.

He shook his head at me and smiled too. "Can we go back down?" He sounded so hopeful.

"Of course," I told him. "I'll take care of you."

He smiled again and winked at me. "I'll count on that."

This time, instead of him putting his hand on my arm or at the small of my back, I placed my palm on his lower back to guide the way, to give him support and any help he might need. I could tell by the way he slumped he really didn't feel well. When I touched his back, he stood straight up for a second, though, as if surprised. He leaned back into my hand very briefly and then relaxed. We waited for the elevator, not talking, not paying attention to the people now, and we finally made our way down where we spent the rest of the evening at a little side café sipping Coke and talking about nothing too deep.

Like a Daughter?

The sun had dropped low in the sky and although darkness hadn't fallen, the temperature had definitely cooled down. A slight breeze blowing through caused me to shiver a little. It was only a little after 8:00, but we still had two and a half hours before time to meet the youth for the fireworks show.

Six Flags again, and David and I spent the day together as we usually did on those trips. We'd been friends for close to five years by this time and were comfortable just hanging out. We rode some rides, but mostly we walked lazily along talking and laughing, watching others' excitement as they rode rides, enjoying seeing kids loving their sno-cones or ice cream or whatever treat they had talked their parents into buying for them. At one point, we spent at least half an hour watching the remote control boats, David yelling encouragement to the little ones driving.

We rode the train, and glided lazily along the river through the Cave ride. All these easy things made the day peaceful and nice.

A marionette stand caught my eye, and I stopped to look at the dangling puppets. David stepped up beside me, "Are you getting cold, Julie?" He'd seen me shiver.

"A little. I'm okay," I answered.

"I'm chilly, too," he said. "What do you think about running over to the motel and getting our jackets before we have to meet the kids and watch the fireworks?"

"Sure," I shrugged. "That'd be fine. I think I'll be okay either way."

71

"Let's do it, then," said David. "I think by 10:30 and fireworks time, we'll be glad we did."

The lady at the little exit booth stamped our hands so that we could get back into the park, and we made our way to the van. It seemed a little weird to be going with David on my own and leaving the kids, but they were scattered anyway. We weren't with them in the park; they wouldn't even know we were gone. Plus, our motel was less than a mile away.

At the motel, I ran to my room first while he waited in the hallway, and I grabbed my Nike warm-up jacket. It was the only one I'd brought. I hadn't really thought about it being chilly. We headed to David's room next.

I stepped into the room behind him as he flipped the light on. He crossed the room and I stayed by the door, standing awkwardly, feeling strange that I was actually in his motel room. We didn't talk as he dug through the suitcase on the floor looking for what he wanted. 'Ah ha," he announced, and he held up a black fleecy pullover. "Got it."

I stood there across the room looking at him, not thinking of anything to say, thinking of how it would be a perfect time for him to kiss me, not that that would ever happen, thinking how cute he was, thinking how much I liked him, knowing that he didn't/wouldn't like me in that same way. He couldn't. I wondered briefly what in the world was wrong with me to think these things, and then I decided I didn't care.

In half a millisecond, David had crossed the room and stood right in front of me. He looked intensely at me like he tended to do. As always, he seemed to see right inside of me.

"Thank you," he said, "for coming with us. I've had a really great time with you."

I nodded and stared back.

He reached out and hugged me. I hugged him back and thought of something to say. "Sure." Without thinking about it, I wrapped my arms tighter around him and for a second, he did the same. I felt him lean closer to me, hug me a little tighter, my mind couldn't think of anything coherent. It only lasted a second, though.

He dropped his arms much too quickly for me, but he didn't step away. We stood, about a half inch apart looking at each other. It still felt awkward, but it was exciting too. I thought…maybe… it certainly felt like a kiss was imminent.

He didn't move. I watched his face, so very close to mine.

In a very low voice he said, "We need to get out of here." And then he added, "Right now."

I nodded again, responding immediately to what he said, and I turned quickly. He reached around me and opened the door for me, following me out, practically pushing me along the way.

I was disappointed, to be honest, despite knowing it shouldn't happen. I really thought he was going to kiss me. Instead, it seemed he didn't want to.

A few days later

After a morning at tennis camp, I stopped by the mailbox on my way in the house. I shuffled through letters as I walked, stopping when I saw David's name in the return address of one of them. Shoving everything else under my arm, I stood right there in the middle of the driveway and ripped open David's letter, excited to hear from him after seeing him only a few days before. Quickly, I scanned over the two page letter trying to see if he'd written anything 'good'. What I considered good wouldn't be written, anyway. I always just kept hoping. Dreamland. What he did write, though. Well, I wasn't sure what I thought about it:

Julie,

    I've finally recovered from our Six Flags trip. After I got home, I mowed the church lawn and got done about 9:30. Wow, was I exhausted.

    You certainly were a real asset to our group this weekend. The kids had a great time as did I, and I hope you enjoyed yourself. You are such a neat person to be with, and I really enjoyed our time together. If I had a daughter, I'd want her to be just like you!

    I sensed a deep desire in you for a deeper commitment to Jesus Christ. I wish we had more time to visit about spiritual things…

Love in Him,
David

A daughter, huh? I felt deflated. For a moment. What did I want most from David, anyway? Daydreaming, I saw us together, a couple. Reality, though, didn't lend itself to that. David had never indicated anything more. A daughter? Ouch. But…I could handle daughter more than I could handle nothing at all. I felt alive with David. He was so much fun, so happy, so joyful. Spending time with him made me feel that way, too. I wouldn't give that up, not even if it meant just being like a daughter. A deep desire for a deeper commitment to Christ? I had to laugh at that one (sorry God). I had just wanted David to kiss me; it didn't go any deeper than that. Whatever David saw in me, I don't know. But it certainly made me think.

Whistling Out the Window

I sat in the window of my dorm room, one leg dangling on the bedroom side and the other curled up under me. My roommate/doubles partner, Jennie, and I removed the screen weeks before so we could more easily harass the passers-by. Because we played on the tennis team, we stayed living in the dorms long past the time many students ventured out into their own apartments. In the beginning, we'd been cautious about our behavior or calling attention to ourselves. By the third year, we didn't really care.

"When's he going to be here?" Jennie asked. She sat on her bed with her biology book open. I knew she only pretended to study. We both hated biology and hoped to get by with some luck and maybe a few cheats here and there. There was no sense in me even pretending to study while I waited for David. I could only think about David.

"He said 5:00, so it will be…"

"4:55," Jennie finished.

I laughed. "Yep, that's right."

Sure enough, at about 5 'til 5:00 I saw his beat up, I-don't-know-how-old, orange Chevy truck pull into the parking lot.

"He's here!"

"You squealed that," Jennie teased me as she jumped up from her bed and ran to join me at the window.

"He's here, he's here, he's here." How stupid could I act?

We watched him park and hop out of his truck. He wore jeans and a dark blue button down short-sleeved shirt. Blue was a good color for him. Blue matched his eyes.

"Wooooooooooowoooooooooooooo!" Jennie and I both yelled down at David, and I added the longest loudest wolf whistle I could.

"Hey there, hey you!" I yelled while Jennie kept wooooowoooooo-ing.

David looked up grinning that huge grin and waved.

"I'll meet you in the lobby," I yelled. And I took off out the door yelling "byeeeee Jennnnnnnie" behind me. We were on the 2nd floor. I ran so fast I was down the two flights of stairs, took them two at a time thankyouverymuch, and in the lobby just as he walked in the front door.

He ran his fingers through the flop of brown hair on his forehead and pushed it back, looked up at me, stopped where he was, and smiled. "Hey, Juliebean."

"Hey, David."

"I have to tell you," he said, "that it does a guy's ego good to have two beautiful college women whistling at him."

Beautiful? Cool. I smiled at him, all of a sudden feeling shy again. No one had ever said I was beautiful before. Oh, I knew David was just saying that, but still.

It felt kind of nice. He smiled so big I could just almost think he meant it. That made me actually feel that way…beautiful, that is. I liked it.

We stood there for a minute staring at each other. Finally, I moved forward. He put his hand at the small of my back as we headed out the door but dropped it when we reached the sidewalk. Darn.

Not saying much but the usual How are yous, we strolled to his truck. I went around to my side to hop in, but he reached out and put his hand on my arm. "Wait a minute, Julie," I could hear the amusement in his voice. "Everyone knows that in Oklahoma when you go on a date in a pick-up truck, you have to get in on the driver's seat and sit reallll close to the driver."

Oh, this was new. Not the info., of course. I knew that about Oklahoma pick-up truck dates. I'd been on a couple. Just that it was a 'date'. Really? And that he wanted me to get in on his side and sit reallll close to him. Man.

I tried to think of something witty to say as I headed back over to his side (because of course I was going to do that). All I could come up with was, "Okay." He held the door, and I kind of ducked under his arm and up into the truck scooting across enough that it wouldn't look like I was desperate to sit in his lap but not so far I couldn't touch him…discreetly, of course.

I glanced over at him still feeling extra shy but also so very thrilled with the whole thing. He caught my eye and held it for just a minute; I was the one who looked away first. One of these days, I was going to outlast him. Not this day, though.

He scooted in next to me, and I felt his thigh press hard against mine. Hmm. I stared straight ahead not daring to do anything else, and off we went on our 'date'.

Date or not, I don't know. If a date includes physicality, then it wasn't a date. If it has to do with conversation and connection, understanding and laughter, then maybe it was. The entire evening raced by; I don't remember the details, not of the conversation. I just remember each specific moment riding in his truck, thigh pressed up against his. Shallow? Maybe. It seemed more than that, but then, who knows? His leg and the occasional brush of my arm or back were the only times he touched me, and I remember being disappointed. What I do know for sure - we had a wonderful time. We talked and laughed and talked some more. I spoke more openly with David than I'd ever spoken with anyone, not silly chatter to make each other laugh but real words, about all that was inside of me. How I felt. What I thought. He never gave an inch when challenging me to think, to contribute. He was direct and expected the same from me. I felt safe talking to David, sharing my dreams and feelings and beliefs. Everything I told him, he listened intently, encouraging me, understanding me. He seemed to value me for just being me. I never did really understand if he meant what he said about a date. He was probably just kidding. I simply didn't know.

No Boy Will Ever Like Me

I grabbed for my napkin but stopped suddenly when David reached out his hand and lay it on top of mine. Picking my fingers up, he ran the pad of his thumb over my index fingernail. I tried to pull my hand away, but he wouldn't let me.

"You bite your nails," he stated, not with any sort of critical tone, just matter-of-factly.

Again I tried to pull back, but he kept my hand, running his thumb over each of my nails now. I was embarrassed, but I didn't want him to know it.

"Yeah." If I acted like I didn't care, maybe it wouldn't matter so much.

"How come?" he asked me.

I shrugged.

We sat for a minute, neither of us speaking. Finally, I shrugged again and then looked away. "I always have. I just do."

He slipped his hand up a little, holding my hand now instead of only my fingers. He didn't speak; he just waited for me.

Feeling shy and insecure, I couldn't look at him. Biting my nails was a habit I'd battled as long as I could remember. I knew they looked ugly; I hated when people noticed.

"My mom told me no boy would ever like me if I didn't stop biting them." I peered up at him then, pretending confidence, as if I didn't care what my mom had told me.

Up went his eyebrows, and he gripped my hand tighter. "You don't believe that, do you, Julie? You don't believe that?"

I met his gaze and slightly shook my head. "No," I whispered. But it wasn't true. Logically, I knew the right guy would like me no matter what, but in my heart I feared Mom was right. I wasn't good enough. My nails were ugly. I wasn't smart enough, motivated enough. Despite the growth my confidence level had made through recent years, those early insecurities from the constant knocking down of my self-esteem continued to take precedence. I fought them every single day.

"Julie," David started, stopped, sighed. Started again. "Julie, she didn't mean it. She was just trying to get you to stop biting your nails and didn't know how to otherwise. She was just trying to…find something that would motivate you to quit. She didn't really mean it. It's not true."

"Okay, David." I nodded, but I didn't believe him.

"It's not true," he repeated slowly, emphasizing each word, his voice raised slightly. "You are more than that. More than fingernails. More than any one thing."

He chuckled then. "No boy will like you, huh? How many boyfriends have you had?"

I shrugged.

"Too many to count, right? Don't lie. You've already told me about them." He teased me, making me laugh. He could always make me laugh, no matter what.

"Nooo."

"Yes," he answered back. "And I can guarantee you they didn't care about your fingernails."

"But none of them lasted," I argued.

"Julie! You broke up with them. Every one of them. Don't deny it; it's true."

I grinned at him and shook my head. "Not really…well, mostly. Not every one," I told him.

He smiled again, "Okay, I'll give you that. Mostly. So you know what your mom said is not true."

"Okay, David." Again, I nodded.

He kept my hand in his and leaned across the table closer to me, making me focus on him. "You are more than that. See yourself through my eyes. You are…so much more than that. Stop letting other people's insecurities affect you and keep you from being all that you are."

I clung to his hand almost as tightly as I clung to his words. I wanted what he said to be true. His words gave me hope - because I trusted him.

"I will, David. I will."

He squeezed my hand. "Promise me. Remember, you are God's creation. You are full of Him – your compassion, your humor, your joy. That's who you are. You promise me you'll remember that."

"I will."

He smiled and added, "And don't worry about fingernails."

I grinned back at him. "I won't."

As soon as he let go of my hand, I curled my fingers back, hiding my nails out of habit. He noticed, though, winked at me, and said, "You promised."

I laughed at him again and spread my hands back out on the table, daring to be confident. I didn't want to bite my nails. I hated the nasty habit but couldn't seem to break it. Not being able to do so didn't make me a bad person. It really didn't. It just made me…me…right? A work in progress. Always.

Mike

"I met a guy," I told David. We sat in his truck eating pina colada sno-cones from a little stand outside of a gas station.

David raised his eyebrows at me, "A guy, huh? Sounds serious."

I laughed. "Not every guy is serious."

"No guy is serious to you, Julie." He smiled and took another bite of his sno-cone.

"This one might be," I told him.

Up went his eyebrows again. "I'd better hear more about him then. Tell me."

"He's really nice. Funny." I stopped, not sure about continuing. I could talk to David about everything, even guys. For some reason, though, it seemed different talking about Mike.

David asked, "Is he cute?"

I reached out and hit him, knowing he was teasing me about my boyfriend requirements from years ago. "Yes!"

He laughed, "He's a keeper, then."

"His name is Mike. He loves Stephen King," I added. "And he's really smart. Almost scary smart."

"You are, too."

I shook my head. "No, not like that. Like, smart, smart. And he's really nice."

"You already said that one. Nice. Is he double nice?"

"David!"

He laughed again. "I'm glad, Julie. I'm glad you met this guy. I hope he understands how special you are."

"Me too." I grinned, looking down into my sno-cone feeling like the old shy Julie like I used to when David would compliment me. No matter how long I'd known him, I was still sometimes in awe of him. He seemed so good to me. I didn't always feel on an even par with him. Insecurities ingrained in me from early years continued to affect my confidence. David's encouragement helped hold that back, though.

Plans for My Future

"You've decided to major in what?" David set his fork down, peering quizzically across the table at me. On my night off, I took him to the upscale barbecue restaurant where I worked. I loved my job hostessing there, loved the people. Going in on a night off to share the place I loved with David seemed natural. Because of the restaurant's history and popularity, David had been there before. However, I could tell him more history, more of the inside scoop. Plus, the bartender/assistant manager, Brian, always snuck a huge discount onto my bill and sent free 'extras' to our table.

Our conversation steered in the direction of my college plans. "Education," I told him.

"What happened to broadcasting?" David still hadn't picked his fork back up. He stared intently at me waiting for me to answer.

"Well, I just plan to add education to my degree," I said. "Communications will still be the main part of it." I paused for a minute and sipped my Coke, thinking David might say something. He just stared, so I continued. "Dad says if I add education that will give me more opportunity in case the broadcasting thing doesn't work out."

I could always tell what David thought by watching his eyebrows. They expressed most every emotion he conveyed. Now, I watched them knit into a skeptical, unsure 'V'. "I see," he said. "Kind of like a fall back plan."

"Right," I nodded at him but looked away not ready for him to challenge me on this.

"Is it what you want?"

"Well, sure, David," I answered. "Why not? I'll still major in communications. Public speaking. And I'll take the education classes, just in case."

David chuckled, "But you love to talk, Julie. Public speaking fits you."

"I know, David," I laughed and tried to sound reassuring. To him and to myself. I really didn't want to pursue an education degree, but Dad thought it would be the right thing, and I valued my Dad's opinion. I also seldom strayed from what he suggested I do, in anything.

Picking up his fork again, David tackled his brisket and sat chewing. I stared at him, not saying anything, waiting for him to finish. Waiting for him to say more.

He took a drink, wiped his mouth with his napkin, and sat back again. Still, I waited.

"Julie," finally, he spoke. "Julie." He said it again. "Do you remember when you told me you wanted to major in Communications?"

I thought back to several years before and remembered our first conversation about my future and what I wanted to accomplish in my life. I nodded at him.

He continued. "I teased you about it, remember? About how shy you are. About how impossibly funny it would be to have somebody so admittedly shy actually major in speaking in front of people."

"I know, David."

"I know, too. You told me about spending every year in school from kindergarten on in the principal's office at least once and usually more for talking too much in class." He laughed a little remembering that, and I did too.

"It's true," I told him.

"Yes, I know." He laughed again, and then went on. "You told me then that while you might struggle to meet new people and to create friendships, that when you talked to people…just talked…that attention to you, that positive response to you, I mean, think about it, you're well-spoken, you're smart, you have things to say that people want to hear..those things made you feel confident. Finally. When nothing else did. You always enjoy talking to people, not in conversation necessarily but in front of them. Positive attention."

"I still feel that way, David."

"So why are you changing your major?"

"I'm not changing it. I'm just adding to it."

He shook his head. "No, you aren't. You're changing it. And that's okay to do if you want it. If you want it, it's the right thing. If you're doing it to fall back on…" he trailed off and got quiet.

"What, David?"

"I just don't want you to use it as an excuse to not go after what you want. You should go for everything you want."

"It'll be fine, David. It's a good idea. That way, if I don't make it in broadcasting or any type of communications, I can still teach speech and drama and make a living." The thought didn't sound that great to me, but I still tried to reassure us both.

He stared at me for a long time, slowly nodded his head. "Okay, Julie. Okay. If you want it, do it."

I didn't want it, but the fear of falling short in a competitive field where success rarely came convinced me I needed to. I smiled my biggest smile at David, pretending I felt confident and sure about my decision. "I do want it. I'm going to do it." I don't think I fooled him for a minute, but he supported me anyway.

Smiling back at me, he winked and said, "Okay then. And now…"

"What, what?"

"More bread!" He reached for the platter of fresh bread our waiter had just brought to our table. Laughing together, we ate bread and switched the conversation to lighter topics. Our table sat back in a little private alcove so we faced no danger of offending other diners with our noise, and I didn't have to worry about the possibility of David peering at people with salt and pepper shaker goggles. Not that I really worried about it. Anyone else, and I would die of embarrassment. David had a way, though, of making all of that mischievous fun all right.

He Kissed Me. Finally.

Cicadas chirred noisily and hopefully covered the sound of my groan as I hoisted myself up onto the top of the swing set. Stuffing myself with barbeque ribs probably wasn't the best idea, but yum. David had taken me out to eat again. I'd seen him five times over the past week, much more than usual. Typically, after eating, we spent hours sitting at our table, probably irritating the waiters, talking and talking. Sometimes, we drove around afterwards and talked. Tonight, though, we ate quickly, and he drove me to a little park I never even knew existed just down the street. Tucked back off the road behind a line of trees, it was secluded and empty of people. Except for us.

I balanced carefully on the top of the swing set and looked down at David. He sat, knees pulled up to his chin, on the edge of the slide, watching me and smiling, his eyes bright and big and crinkled up on the edges.

Looking down at him, seeing him smile at me like that, my heart swelled. Corny, I know, but there it was. How else do you describe it? I loved the way his eyes squinted up at me. So cute. Such a huge joyful smile. He made me feel just plain good, about him, about life, and most of all, about myself. I looked at it..at us..from the outside. I couldn't quite 'get' that he really could like me. But he must, right? Why else would he spend so much time with me? I never told him how much he meant to me. I just always made sure I was available to see him any time he called me. So much for playing hard to get.

"What do you think, Juliebean?" he called up to me.

I shifted around and settled myself on the bar, making sure I wouldn't wobble. "About what?"

"Anything. Tell me what you're thinking."

"I don't know. Nothing really."

"I don't believe that."

No way would I tell him what I was thinking. How's this – I'm thinking I'm crazy about you, David. I'm thinking your smile is the most gorgeous thing I've ever seen. I'm thinking I don't know what to do with you. I don't know what to do with us. I don't know how you feel about me or what I'm supposed to do with how I feel about you. I'm thinking….

"It's true. I'm just sittin' here."

"Slide down here."

Laughing all the way, I worked my way across the pole to the top of the slide, scooting along carefully until I reached it. I slid to him and just as I reached the bottom, he was all of a sudden standing up holding his arms out to me to catch me. Laughing together we fell back against the bench banging down on it, laughing some more, talking…about everything. And nothing. I don't remember those details; I just remember how it felt to be there with him. I remember the feeling of being with him.

***

Too quickly, it was time to go. It was well past 10:00 p.m., and he had an hour and a half drive to get home. David opened the car door for me, such a gentleman, and I slid into the seat brushing past him on the way. He stood up very straight and waited for me to get settled before slamming the door. I watched him walk around the front of the car and laughed a little when he all of a sudden got taller from walking along the curb. I kept watching him all the way to his door, seeing him open it, watching him bend and get in. He hadn't looked at me yet, but I kept staring at him ready to smile when he finally did.

Instead, he totally took me by surprise. He sat, turned toward me, and in one motion leaned over and kissed me. Just like that. His lips were on mine, and he kissed me. He kissed me.

He pulled back just an inch, searching my face intensely. "Is that okay," he whispered at me, almost frantic. "Is it alright?"

I said what immediately came to mind. "Wow." I nodded. "Yes."

He kissed me some more.

Gebel Sweetness

"Here's the living room. Duh, I know. Kinda obvious." I walked David through my new condo. I'd just moved to a bigger place with three other girls. "The kitchen..." I nodded my head in the right direction.

"Who's this?" He reached down and picked up my cat.

"Oh, that's Gebel. Is that okay? Do you like cats? You're not allergic?"

He held her close and rubbed under her chin. She purred so loudly I could hear her. "She's happy." He laughed. "I love cats."

"Do you have any?" I asked him.

"No." He shook his head, cuddled her closer. "I want a dog, though. Some day."

"Get one now."

"I can't now." His voiced trailed off, and he was quiet for a second. "Some day," he repeated.

"Gebel's a different kind of name. Where'd it come from?" She started pushing against him ready to jump out of his arms, so I reached out for her.

"Gunther Gebel-Williams. From the circus," I added as I could see his confused look. "He's the animal trainer."

David nodded his head, grinned. "You like the circus?"

"Love it."

"What do you love about it?"

Gebel settled into my arms, and I pulled her to me, feeling her soft fur and listening to her still loud purr. I kissed her head.

"I don't know. It's exciting. And free. It makes me feel free."

"Like carefree?" He asked, grinning at me. But he wasn't making fun of me. He was...I don't know. Just listening to me.

I nodded.

"I get that, Julie. I understand."

I smiled at him. I didn't tell many people how much I loved the circus. Oh, those closest to me knew, but I didn't offer the information to just anyone.

"I watched Gunther once in between shows. I snuck back there where they take care of the animals, and I watched him work. He was like the star, and instead of having someone else do the hard work, he did it; he packed together all the meat for the tigers. For every single tiger, he stopped and talked to them as he put their food down. And I swear it looked like they listened to him. It was so cool. He seemed so kind." I shook my head. "I know that's weird. I just loved him because of his glamour, and then I saw him with such compassion."

"That's pretty neat."

"Yeah," I continued. "I met him. Got my picture taken with him. I was so happy that I showed my mom; she rolled her eyes. Said he was a disgusting little old man."

David rolled his eyes at that, and I giggled at the sight. I'd never seen him roll his eyes at anyone, and the thought of him rolling his at my mom rolling hers. Well. "She didn't see the compassion you saw. Didn't want to realize there might be anything deeper inside of him."

"No."

"Seems like she often misses that in people."

I buried my face in Gebel's fur so my voice was muffled. "Gebel's my baby. Aren't you, Gabe?" I peeked over her long white fur and saw him watching me.

Neither of us spoke for what seemed like forever.

He finally broke the silence. "You're so sweet." He reached over, brushing his knuckles lightly against my cheek.

"Nah." I shook my head, shrugged off his words.

"Maybe you're so sweet because you don't realize it?" He was laughing at me again.

I laughed back at him this time. "I don't think so, David."

Feeling Stagnant

We drove out of the city away from its many-colored glaring lights and into the darkness of the countryside. I had no idea where we were going, if anywhere at all. David drove and drove turning down this road and that. I sat and watched his hands grip the steering wheel. His hands fascinated me even while merely driving. They were so strong and firm. I thought about them playing his guitar, the piano. And I thought about holding his hand, how it felt, his fingers wrapped around mine. Yes, holding his hand was a whole experience in itself. The energy that rushed from his palm into mine, up my arm and into me, every nerve on fire. Mm.

David was telling me a story and making me laugh. "You are so funny," I told him, looking over at him, thinking how full I felt when I was with him. He felt like another part of me. I'd never felt anything like that before. Never. I didn't know I could feel like that before David. Oh, I'd heard all the romantic stories, but I just thought that was a choice a person made. I'd no idea you just got swept up in it and had no control at all. That was tough for someone hell bent on being in control all the time.

"It's rich, isn't it?" David said.

"What?"

"That's what my dad says when he thinks I'm funny, 'Oh, David, that's rich.'" He said it in a deep voice, imitating how his dad must have sounded.

I laughed. "That's perfect."

"I know." He smiled, and I could see the love he felt for his dad in his expression, but I could see something else, too. He seemed almost distant, like something else distracted him. I'd never seen him that way before.

Reaching over, I lay my hand on his arm. He let go of the steering wheel, and I slid my hand down, taking his in mine.

"What's the matter, David?" I asked him, worried at what I might hear. I couldn't even imagine what it might be. It wasn't what I expected.

"I think I'm going to leave my church," he answered. He was still driving. We had been going up and down back roads, and I had no idea where we were.

"You do?"

He nodded.

"Why, David?"

"I'm not sure I know how to explain," he started, and then he stopped because at that moment he looked at me again for a bit too long and when he looked back at the road, he had to jerk the car back into our lane.

I gripped his hand tighter, lending my support. "Maybe we should find someplace to stop so we can talk about it."

He caressed my hand with his thumb but didn't look at me again. "I'd like that," he said.

We drove in silence the next few minutes as he looked for someplace to pull over. It was so dark; there were no house lights anywhere. Finally, we saw a small gravel area to the side of the road. David swung the car in and put it in park, leaving the engine running. He turned toward me, and I scooted closer to him, leaning in to him. I barely had time to register how serious his expression before he kissed me, gently. I was worried about that look on his face. I broke away and lay my head on his chest listening for his heartbeat.

"Tell me," I whispered, almost afraid to hear what he was going to say.

His fingertips circled around and around my back tracing grooves through my shirt into my skin. He didn't speak at first. Gathering his thoughts, I guessed. Sitting there, resting against him, feeling him stroke my back…I wasn't in any hurry.

"I feel," he paused, leaned to kiss me again, this time on my forehead, started again, "disillusioned by my church."

"How do you mean?" I whispered.

'Round and 'round he still caressed my back, and I lay there against him mesmerized by the sound of his voice, trying hard to catch every word, every part of him. This time I heard his concerns, his problems, instead of it being the other way around. Usually, I was the one pouring my heart out to him. I only hoped I could support him in the same way he always did me. I wasn't used to being the strength in our relationship.

He talked to me about the people in the church and how frustrated he was that while they talked about loving Jesus, they never seemed to live that way. They didn't do anything, really. Just came to church and left church each Sunday.

"They're stagnant, Julie," he said. "Knowing Christ's love, truly knowing it, you can't help but be motivated to do something. I just don't understand. I don't understand why people don't get it."

I wished I had all the answers for him. Unfortunately, I didn't have any answers at all. I heard his words, heard the feeling behind them, but I didn't understand the motivation of Christ's love. Didn't we simply do things because we were supposed to? I didn't really understand any other way. I did understand that it was important to David, and because it was, I kept listening. I have to admit, though, I did have the fleeting thought of enough talk and more kissing. That was pretty much the extent of where my brain was.

David sat up a little straighter and pulled me even closer to him until I was almost in his lap. He shifted to keep the steering wheel from gouging us both and then completely wrapped his arms around me. I felt his lips against my ear, and I shivered. He whispered, and I could barely hear what he said, "I just don't understand, and so I would like to find someplace where I can relate a little better."

I nodded. I knew how big this was for him, the importance he placed on his church. He was no longer a youth director and hadn't been for well over a year. Instead, he'd secured a full time position as executive director of a known charitable organization. The newspapers called him a 'local businessman' now. Still, his church remained an essential part of his life.

"There's a difference, you know," he said, "a difference in living for Jesus and allowing Jesus to live through you."

I thought about that for a minute, and for only that minute it made perfect sense to me. Living for Jesus meant living from the outside in, doing things merely for the sake of doing them whether it was for appearances or maybe because we thought that by doing the good deeds we could be closer to Jesus. But allowing Jesus to live through us…by doing that, we would truly be living from the inside out, knowing the love within us that is Christ and allowing it to pour out of us into the world. That would definitely motivate a person to do things.

"I understand what you mean, David," I told him.

He cupped my chin in his hand and then ran his palm up the side of my cheek. "I knew you would," he said, and he kissed me again. I didn't think about that conversation again for a long time. That night, I understood. In the years after, I didn't really remember to remember it. I mean, I remembered the occasion. I just didn't remember the meaning behind what he said. He was struggling, and instead of following through and making sure he was okay, I focused on his kisses and what he might feel about me.

Field of David

"Ouch!" I yelped, still giggling a little even though pointy pasture grass poked into the pad of my foot. The grass had worked its way up into my sandals as we trekked across the idontknowhowmanyacre field to get to the towering oak we spotted from the car and determined a perfect picnic place. The summer had been so dry, the grass was stiff and prickly, and it surprised me when it stuck into my skin.

I grabbed David's arm to help balance myself as I pulled my right foot up and tried to dig around under my sandal straps to pull out the offending blades of grass. Something brushed against the top of my head, and then I felt David's breath in my ear. "Better than stepping in that pile of manure, right, Juliebean?" he whispered. I shivered despite the fact that it was easily in the 90s out. I reacted that way to David. Still. Always. I tried to keep that from him, though. No sense in letting him know just how much he affected me. That would mean giving up some control and feeling vulnerable, and I wasn't sure I was up for that. He'd made no commitment to me, and while I didn't care to admit it aloud, I had to prepare myself for the end. The end always lurked around in the back of my mind threatening to ruin my happiness. He had another life. Another world. One I wasn't a part of. I thought about it all the time when we were apart but never asked him when we were together. I could now, but I was too scared to know.

Besides, now wasn't the time to worry about it.

"Sandals in a pasture? Seriously?" he whispered again, teasing me as usual, laughing at me.

"Heyyy," I protested his tease letting go of his arm just long enough to playfully punch him. Unfortunately, I failed to remember that I still only stood on one foot, and I immediately began to topple over. "Ack," I flailed wildly reaching for his arm. Instead of letting me grab it, he slung it around my waist, squeezing me tight and holding me up, pressed against his side for extra support.

"I've got you, Julie," he assured me, laughing still. I glanced up at him, feeling a little silly and wanting to come back with some smart comment. When I saw his face, though, his smile directed at me, those blue eyes staring at me, I lost all train of thought. I could only stare back. David's expression changed, just for that moment.

All of a sudden he looked serious. Intense. I wasn't sure exactly what it meant. Well, I thought I knew what it might mean, but I couldn't imagine that. I couldn't imagine that David might really feel about me the same way I felt about him. I had to pretend I didn't care. I was too cool to care. How could I truly invest in us when I didn't really have a say? I knew what I was doing was wrong, but I couldn't stop myself. Sometimes, I'd catch a look on his face I wondered about. Like he was just about to say something, and then he wouldn't. I kept thinking I'd ask him about that, too, but I never did. I was too scared to know what he might say, too afraid whatever he said would take him away from me.

I started to look away. Before I could, I heard a thunk as he dropped the bag he'd been holding in his other hand. I didn't have time to think, much less do anything before he pulled me around to face him and stepped very close to me.

Words escaped me. That was actually for the best, and I should have gone with that and stayed quiet, but I was too nervous to stand there and stare. David was so big to me, so all-encompassing. He always had been. Briefly I wondered if I would ever get used to his presence and intensity. "Hi," I smiled up at him.

He grinned but didn't answer. Instead, he leaned even closer, and I felt his mouth on my cheek. Very soft. Unexpected.

"Oh," I breathed out. I felt his hand trail up my back, into my hair, gently pulling me against his chest. He wrapped his other arm tighter around me, securing me closer. He rested his cheek atop my head, and I lay against him with my ear pressed against his chest listening to the thump, thump of his heart. We stood that way, not talking, actually quiet for once, one of his hands gently entwined in my hair, his other arm encircling me, holding me close. A slight breeze blew past providing a bit of relief from the stifling heat and bringing with it the smell of freshness and summertime. I closed my eyes and just, felt.

It was quite a while before we made it the rest of the way across the field to set up our picnic under the old oak. We had all the time in the world to get to that…all the time to stand together holding each other. That's how it felt, anyway.

Bully Mom

I heard the chatter of my roommates in the living room of the apartment we shared. They were behind me, wrapped up in their own conversation, seemingly not paying any attention to me at the open door. David stood at the bottom of the porch stairs gazing up at me. He smiled, and something inside me in the pit of my stomach flipped over and then filled me completely full of him. It had been a week since I'd last seen him. I had no idea what he'd been doing during that time and had only talked to him once late on Tuesday when he called me from his office when he'd had to work late. Desperate to be in control of my life and our relationship, I was determined not to let on that I'd missed him, that I'd thought about him every moment. I stood up straighter, attempting confidence, as if he didn't really affect me. I was cool. So cool. I smiled back at him and waved. "Hi." I called out. He held his hand out to me, reaching up the stairs towards me. I couldn't hear the girls any more. I'm sure they were still there chattering away but I only focused on David. Smiling, I took a deep breath hoping to stop shaking so he wouldn't notice how much he affected me. Still. "Hey Julie," he said to me, and I stepped forward and took his hand. He pulled me down close to him and gave me a quick hug but dropped his hand. And his arm. We no longer touched. I wanted to touch him again, but I was too scared. What if he didn't want me to? What if he thought it was dumb, if I didn't do it right?

Without thinking I reached out anyway, brushing my fingers alongside his upper arm. He stopped and turned to me. I looked away but then back again, trying still to seem confident even though I was the farthest from it I could be. "I just…"

David did the same, brushed his fingers along my arm and then down, all the way down to my hand where he let his fingers lace between mine. "You ready?" He smiled down at me, and I could only nod. The feel of his hand in mine distracted me and made me forget anything else I wanted to say.

I tripped over the last porch step out the door but caught myself before I went over. "Super," I laughed. He laughed at me, too, and pulled me around to him, wrapping his arms around me. He leaned down, and I felt his breath on my neck and then in my ear as he whispered to me, "I'm so glad to see you. I've missed you." And then off we went to climb into his truck. By the way, I got in on the driver's side and sat reeeeal close to the driver.

***

I shook my head and gripped his hand a little tighter taking comfort in the strength of his grip. "I don't know, David," I told him. "I don't know why she's so mean to me. I don't know what I've done to cause her to criticize me every time I turn around."

We were talking about my stepmother, of course. I'd made the apparent mistake of wearing the wrong shoes to church when I'd gone home the past weekend. "You're not wearing those with that dress are you?" she'd rolled her eyes up and made the gasp I knew too well. Mom always made it very clear what she thought of my choices. I could never please her, but I kept trying.

I sighed and leaned my head against David's shoulder, frustrated with my mother, frustrated with my reaction to her and my inability to keep her from bothering me, relieved to be somewhere with someone where I felt safe. And strong.

He loosened his fingers from mine and wrapped his arm around me pulling me closer. I felt his lips brush the top of my head. They tickled when he spoke. "Have you considered she criticizes you to make herself feel better?" he asked me.

I didn't answer and he went on, "She's a bully, Julie. She reminds me of the classic schoolyard bully. Haven't you ever noticed that when you stand up to her she backs down? She's trying to intimidate you. That's what she does."

It was true. David was right. It was so hard for me, though, to remember that in the moment. 22 years old and I still reverted back to a small child when it came to reacting to my mother's criticism.

"She makes me feel like I'm not good enough. Every day. I thought when I moved away, I'd be through having to feel this way, but even when I don't talk to her, the memory of her and what she would say to me makes me feel the same." I cried out. "I hate it."

David held me close whispering in my ear, "Let it go, Julie. Let it go. You can't change her."

"What if she's right?" I whispered back at him. "What if I'm not good enough for her. What if I'm never good enough for her?"

"What if you aren't?"

I had no answer for that. I wasn't sure what he meant, so I just sat, waiting.

He repeated it. "What if you aren't? Julie, consider this - you'll never be good enough for her because it's not really about you. It's about her. She only wants you to think it's about you."

I shook my head.

He pulled me in closer and whispered in my ear again, "Let that feeling go. What she tries to make you feel doesn't matter. It isn't what's real. Don't worry. I'm here. You have me. You are good enough. You're more than good enough. It'll be okay. You'll be okay."

But I didn't really. I didn't have him. When he took me back to my apartment, he'd drive home. 90 miles to his wife. We didn't talk about that. We never did.

A Guitar Promise

We sat in a little bar right off of Broadway Extension. It was late. Low lights hung inside darkening the room and creating intimacy despite the loud music blaring through the speakers. Our chairs pressed so close together side by side, though, we could see and hear each other perfectly. I don't remember what the music was that played in the background. Other people were there, but I don't remember how many.

I sat on his right, leaning against him. Very gently, I touched the inside of his thigh with my fingertips feeling the denim rough against my skin, his leg hard and firm underneath my touch. Slowly, I slid my fingers down and pressed my palm flat feeling him tense for a moment and then relax. I peeked up at his face. His eyes were partially closed. He took a deep breath and met my gaze. "Hi," he said, his voice low. "Hi," I smiled up at him watching his face closely. He closed his eyes again, pursed his lips and blew out just a little breath. I'd seen that expression on his face before both when we touched and when he played his guitar. Such a peaceful, content look. I wondered at that look, that he had it for me.

Keeping my left hand on the inside of his thigh, I reached over with my right and lay my palm against his cheek feeling the beard scruff I loved so much. He opened his eyes and reached up, putting his hand over mine.

"What do you think about all of this, Julie?" he still held my hand pressed against his cheek.

"About what, David?"

"This. Us."

I took a minute to think how I wanted to answer. Coming up with the words to describe my feelings was impossible.

"I don't know, David. It's…wonderful. It's….right. I don't kn…"

He sat up straighter and shifted in his seat to face me better, pulling our still connected hands into his lap.

"It is right, isn't it?" he said, tilting his head toward me. I answered by lowering mine so that my forehead rested against his.

"Yeah," I said. I took a deep breath, thinking about the look on his face – the me look, the guitar look. "God, I had such a crush on you from the very beginning," I admitted to him.

He sat back for a second and looked at me surprised. "You did?"

I had thought it obvious all those years ago.

"Oh yeah," I said. "From the very start. The very first time I saw you. You were up on the mantel playing your guitar." I squeezed his hands a little tighter. "I used to love to watch you play your guitar."

"Really?"

I nodded.

"I haven't played my guitar in ages."

"I loved watching you. Listening to you play and sing."

He leaned his head back against mine and in his low voice he whispered just loud enough for me to hear him over the music, "I never knew that."

"It's true," I told him.

"As soon as I can, I'll get my guitar back out and play for you."

I breathed him in and put my hands back up to his face. I loved to feel his face. With my lips right on his, I told him, "I would really love that." Very softly, I kissed him.

Suicide and Dreams

"Where do you want to go?" he asked me. His grin had begun. Spreading wider. He blinked at me dramatically...one long, pronounced blink and then popped his eyes wide at me. Then just sat there. Staring.

My heart jumped - no, not from love, just from nerves. It had to simply be nerves - then, it pounded wildly as I tried to think of something to answer. Where did I want to go? Who cared? David could take me out behind the sewage plant on an evening when the wind blew just right, sit me down next to him, look at me once, smile...and my day would be complete. Sewage smell and all. Okay, so maybe that's an exaggeration. But not really.

At any rate, I didn't know how to answer him. I shrugged and tried desperately to maintain eye contact. I think I did okay, but trying to keep up with David was tough. Briefly, I wondered for the millionth time what he saw in me. He was perfect. Incredible. And I was...me.

He touched his fingertips to my temple and lightly brushed them into my hair. His palm grazed my cheek as he trailed his fingers through my hair, wrapping them gently around the back of my head. I leaned into his hand and closed my eyes.

"I don't care where we go, David," I whispered to him. He didn't answer and so after a minute I peeked up at him. His eyes were closed, too. He must have felt me shift around because he looked at me then and smiled again. His expression surprised me. He looked dreamy. And content. I still didn't understand it.

He brushed his thumb across my lower lip. I sat very still.

"I want you to choose, Julie."

"Let's just go back to the apartment and talk. We can watch TV." I couldn't think of anything else I really wanted to do. He always came up with great ideas - the botanical garden, the zoo, a walk in the park - I could only think of TV. Go me.

***

The TV droned on in the background neither of us paying much attention to it. At all. I sat so close to David I might as well have been on his lap, my leg draped over his and my arms wrapped around him. I never felt like I could get close enough to him. It was like I needed to be inside of him, and I'm not talking about sex either.

I told him about it once, about how I felt about that. After I'd said it, I glanced away from him as fast as I could afraid I'd said something too stupid or too weird. He took my chin, though, and made me look back at him. He didn't say anything, just stared with that look he got when he was thinking about us. Oh, he didn't have to tell me he was thinking about us. I knew. I just never could tell exactly 'what' he was thinking about us, and that's what drove me crazy. So he got that look again and then the right side of his mouth turned up in a little half grin. I simply stared back at him, unsure what to do or say, still wondering if he would laugh at me at the outrageous thing I'd just admitted to him. Instead, he wrapped me up in his arms, pulling me tight against him. He kissed the top of my head and then rested his chin where his lips had just been. I don't know what he was thinking, but I didn't really care. I pressed every part of myself up against him, from shin to thigh, waist, stomach, chest, arms wrapped around him, cheek resting on his chest. As close as I was to him, he pulled me even closer, locking his arms around me. We'd stood there a very long time, but he never said a word. Just held me until some time later when we slowly separated and made our way to the kitchen to make cookies. It wasn't long until we were laughing as we baked, being silly, singing along to the radio…and we didn't talk about what had happened.

And there I was again, pressed against him as tightly as I could. His right arm squeezed me close to his side, and without thinking about it I pressed my lips against his neck, under his ear. I breathed him in and could smell his cologne. His skin felt a little rough under my lips. I heard him take a deep breath.

"I had the weirdest dream the other night," I whispered into his neck. Why I brought up a dream at that very moment is beyond me.

"About me?" I could hear the humor in his tone even though he didn't actually laugh out loud. But it was good, you know? A good kind of humor that made me feel full. And included.

"No, not this time." I teased him back but then sat up a little straighter because the seriousness of my dream came back to me.

"It was about my mother."

"Good dream or bad dream?"

"Good, I think. I didn't talk to her, but I saw her. It felt peaceful.

"David?" I asked him. "Do you think it was real? Was it really her? I've heard of people being visited in their dreams. Do you think she could be peaceful or is it just something I hope for?"

He sat up straighter, too, nodding slightly as he answered me. "I don't know if the dream was real or not if by real you mean her spirit visiting you. I don't know what I think about that. But I do believe she can be peaceful."

"Even though she killed herself?"

He nodded and pulled me back to him. "I have a hard time imagining a God who refused to be merciful to someone in pain, someone with mental illness, who didn't understand any other way out. My God would never forsake someone like that."

I thought about his words. They made sense to me, but I just wasn't sure. Church always told us suicide was a sin. An unforgivable one. I couldn't stand the thought of my mother being in hell. I wanted to know the God David talked about. I wasn't sure if he meant it or was just trying to make me feel better. I could see either being true.

"Thank you." Whichever it was, I loved him for it. It was more than I could think about longer than a few moments at a time. My brain still didn't like to go too deep for too long.

Come See Me

Hello," I grabbed up the phone on the sixth ring afraid it was David and I would miss him.

"Julie? Daaaaaave." He always did that, said his name that way when he called. As if I wouldn't know it was him. Ha.

"Hi, David!"

"Hi." His voice had gotten soft.

Pressing my shoulder against my ear to hold the phone in place I dug through the closet to find something to cover up with. I grabbed a yellow beach towel and wrapped it around me. Then, I settled back onto my bed propping my pillow up behind me for support.

"What are you doing?" he asked.

"I just got out of the shower."

There was a tiny moment of silence and then he responded, "Mmm."

"David!"

He laughed. Then, out of the blue, he said, "Come see me, Julie."

"What?" I was surprised. He'd never asked me to go to him before.

"Come see me. Let me show you where I work. Let me show you my town."

I didn't know what to say, so I hesitated. He said again," Come down here. I'd like to see you."

"I don't know, David." I didn't know how to explain it to him. If I went there, then I had to face the reality of his life there. Why would he even ask me to go there? I had no idea. It made no sense to me. Rather than ask him, though, I just stayed silent. Finally, I just said again, "I don't know."

What in the world was wrong with me that I couldn't explain how I felt to him. I could tell him everything, but I just couldn't talk about how scared I was of his other world – a world I didn't belong to.

His voice was still kind. He didn't sound mad or anything when he said, "It's okay, Julie. I understand. I hope someday you'll come."

You Mean More to Me

I sat on the edge of my bed gripping David's recent letter tight. "You mean more to me than I ever believed possible," he had written. "I spend each moment away from you waiting to get back to you."

What did that mean? Did it mean he loved me? Why couldn't he just say those words? And why couldn't I take what he did write at face value? Did I have to have specific words? I knew the way he looked at me, the way he touched me, the way he talked to me. If his behavior and mannerisms around me didn't convey love, I don't know what did. But for some reason I was hung up on hearing the words and because he never said them, because I never heard (or read), Julie, I love you, I thought it couldn't possibly be true. I was so insecure, I couldn't see. I was so afraid of being wrong, I couldn't accept.

Running my finger lightly over the words in his letter, it occurred to me that David's handwriting was just like him. He wrote in all caps, strong bold strokes. Each letter tilted forward as if they couldn't wait to move forward, to go on to the next great adventure. David reminded me of that – bold and strong – always going and going – accomplishing great and meaningful things in everything that he did. I zigzagged my finger down the page to his signature and touched his name at the bottom of the page feeling almost like I was touching him. His signature told so much about him, too, the D signed with huge flourish. It was a signature that shouted out hey, look at me. I had to grin a little and shake my head as I thought how much like David that was. And then there was me. Meek little me. Surely the things he'd written were just words. He didn't mean them. He couldn't. Why would he?

After sitting and contemplating a while longer, I folded the letter back and slipped it into its envelope. Just as with the first letter he'd written me years ago and all the letters in between, this one was just for me, and I wanted to tuck it away in the little box I kept all of the things David gave me in. I wonder sometimes now if I'd shared those letters with anyone, my sister or with Jennie, if I'd had a better perspective, I might have been able to fully accept David's love. Even so, though, what good would that have done? How our relationship ever moved forward wasn't really up to me, was it?

It's Goodbye

Slowly, I hung up the phone thinking about what I'd just agreed to. Mike, the double nice, intelligent,

Stephen King fan, offered to take me to the movie after his work shift ended, and I figured why not. Over the last year, I'd been seeing him more and more. Mike was steady. He was there for me. He wanted to be with me and let me know it frequently. I liked him. He really was super smart, funny, and much kinder than he gave himself credit for. I never wondered how he felt about me, and while I didn't feel the same about him as I felt about David, I enjoyed being with him. We had plenty in common - our love of reading, of Stephen King, of puzzles, and of humor - not always the same type of humor, but still, we loved to laugh. I thought I could probably love Mike, and if he was a little rough around the edges, so what? I could smooth those edges out. What was love anyway? Storybook love wasn't real. I wasn't quite sure what romantic love was. Love just seemed to be whatever you made of it. I thought I loved David. I mean, loved him, loved him. And I hadn't heard from him in almost a month. He'd stopped by a few weeks before with a Christmas gift for me, a book I'd been wanting about The Rolling Stones. I didn't know what was happening with him. His world was not one I was a part of until he was ready. So how is that love? I think, if I'd called him, he would have come to me. But I didn't call him. I wanted him to make that move. Stubborn, I guess, I don't know. It wasn't really my place to call him. Was it?

The phone rang again, and I grabbed it wondering if Mike had different plans.

"Julie?"

"Hi, David." hearing his voice brought a flood of emotion. And of comfort. Of home. I'm not sure if that makes sense, but it's how I felt. I hadn't heard him in so long, I doubted him because of it, and now hearing him made me feel complete and okay again. At least to a point. In my heart. Logically, though, I couldn't get past the fact that he hadn't called. I was so confused and unsure.

"How are you?" he asked.

"I'm good, David." I didn't know what else to say. I wanted to say where have you been, why haven't you called, I've missed you. I didn't say any of those things, though. I don't know why. I just couldn't say anything else. Just...I'm good, David.

"I had a break today and wanted to call," he said.

"Okay." It felt awkward now.

"I've missed you, Julie."

"David, I," I trailed off.

Silence.

I tried again. "David, we need to talk."

"I'll be right there." He'd told me that a million times. This time it was so different.

"Okay," I whispered. He'd already hung up.

I looked at my clock. 2:45. It was an hour and a half drive for him to get to my apartment, so it would be close to dinner time when he arrived. I wanted to call him back, to tell him not to come. I knew he'd already left, though. Besides, I did want him to come. I wanted to see him. God, I wanted to be with him. But he hadn't called. In over three weeks, close to a month, he'd never called me. Was I an afterthought? Was I just someone he wanted to be with when it was convenient for him? I didn't know. I didn't know.

I sat on the couch and reached for the remote. Maybe TV would help me relax while I waited. No such luck. I was too nervous. I turned the TV back off and just sat, waiting. Finally, the minutes passed.

He drove his truck, the old orange 'get in on the driver's side and sit real close to the driver' truck. I loved that truck. I went around to the passenger side and let myself in. David didn't say anything. I scooted part way to him. Kind of close. I still wasn't sure what kind of visit this was. I still wasn't sure his feelings for me. It had been so long. Everything had happened so fast, and then...nothing.

Why we didn't stay at my apartment, I don't know. Instead, we drove into the city. I watched David's hands. He gripped the wheel tightly, but I could still see the tremor in his fingers. He was shaking. Just a little, but I noticed it. I didn't know what it meant.

I don't remember what we talked about while we drove. Not much, if anything. It wasn't important. At some point, David pulled into the parking lot of some big business building, and he parked the truck. He turned slightly to me but kept his hands tight on the steering wheel. I saw they were still shaking. I wondered if he was nervous, too.

"I guess we need to talk, David," I told him.

He nodded. "I guess we do." He let go of the steering wheel and took my hands in his. Then, I could feel them shake.

"David." I paused. I had so much I wanted to say to him. I'd practiced it in my mind over and over. We had so much we needed to discuss. There was so much to say.

"I can't do this anymore. See you."

He dropped my hands and looked down at his lap. I looked down, too. I couldn't look at him. But I wanted his hands back. I wanted David back.

"I understand," he said. "I…" he started something else and stopped. His voice was shaky, unsure. I waited, but he didn't continue.

After a moment, he reached over and started the truck. "Do you want me to take you home?"

"You can just drop me at the restaurant." I was talking about the restaurant where Mike was finishing his shift. I had David take me to Mike's restaurant. What was I thinking? Obviously, I wasn't.

We drove without speaking. The last thing I said to him was, "Thanks. Goodbye."

"Bye, Julie," he said. And that was it.

What happened? What just happened? I had so much I wanted to talk to him about. What did I tell him? I wanted to tell him David, what is going on with us? How do you feel about me? What do I mean to you? David, why haven't you called me? What is our future? What can it be? David, I love you.

I wanted to tell him all of those things. Those things were all in my head waiting to be said. And what I said was "I can't do this anymore…see you."

I stood outside the restaurant before I went in to Mike. Steady, always there, Mike. Fairytale love wasn't real. What just happened proved it. David didn't fight for me. He didn't argue. He didn't try to convince me otherwise. He just said, "I understand."

Love was what you made of it. You love someone and you make things happen. You make love happen. You just, do it yourself.

My heart started to race, my thoughts to panic. I took a deep breath and blocked it out. Unconditional love? Romantic love? That kind of love couldn't be real. If it were, David would love me that way, too. And he didn't. Never once did he say he loved me. I wrapped all that inside of me and tucked it far away where it wouldn't affect me, took another deep breath, and stepped inside to a different future than I'd imagined.

I only ever saw David once more after that, just two months after our 'breakup'. Our mutual friend, Kevin, returned from Desert Storm, and Mike and I went to his welcome home party. David was there. He sat on the floor against the wall, smoking a cigarette. I'd never seen him smoke before. I walked across the room holding Mike's hand. David watched us. I stopped and looked at him. My heart pounded. I knew he had gone back to his own life to live happily ever after, and so I was going to show him that I was also happy with my life. I smiled as broadly as I could and clung tighter to Mike's hand. With the other, I lifted my hand in a wave. "Hi."

He nodded at me, his face serious. "Hi, Julie."

He looked so sad. I wondered why. He reached over and put his cigarette out in a nearby ashtray. His hands were shaking again. What was that all about? I didn't understand it, so I ignored it. Still holding Mike's hand, we walked on by.

Mike told me later about something David said, something bitter and sarcastic about a famous musician. Mike laughed about it, but I wondered. David was never bitter or sarcastic. It just didn't fit who he was.

Random times throughout the years…

"I miss David," I would think to myself. I should call him.

The phone would ring. "Hello."

"Julie? Daaaaaaave."

I Want to See…

"David, I want to see…" I didn't even finish the sentence, and he said, "I'll be right there."

"90 minutes?" I asked, laughing.

"Or faster if I don't get caught."

And again…

"David, I want to see…" I didn't even finish the sentence, and he said, "I'll be right there."

And again…

"David, I want to see…" I didn't even finish the sentence, and he said, "I'll be right there."

PART THREE: I Want to Die, Too

I'm a Grown-Up

Lost in thought, I drove on auto-pilot out Highway V towards our old country house where we'd lived for the past year. The previous October, Mike and I celebrated our 11th anniversary. Three kids and three states later, we'd ended up living in a dilapidated house not far outside of the mid-size Missouri town where we'd moved three years before. Before that, we spent four years in New Mexico teaching on the Navajo reservation and before that, we'd been in Oklahoma City.

Married life with Mike had been full of work and kids and chores. Mike was a good husband and an even better dad. I had no complaints really. For some reason, though, I never felt like I could connect with my life. Oh, don't get me wrong. I loved my children and took care of them - read to them, listened to them, gave them baths, took them places, taught them. But in so much of what I did I felt almost like I was on stage, performing. I lived from the outside of myself trying to do the right things and wondering why I had lost my joy.

When younger, I wanted everything; I wanted to experience it all. I remembered David telling me on the Spinnaker at Six Flags to embrace life. To live it. When Mike and I dated early in our relationship, I tried to explain how I felt to him.

"I want it all. I don't want to 'just' be a teacher. I want to live and experience all I can. I want adventure. I want to dream and do and live and be."

Mike sat and listened and looked blankly at me. He shook his head. "I don't get it." He told me.

I just felt so much. I burned up with the energy and desire to do something, and Mike didn't understand. David would have. I knew that but never said it. It didn't matter now anyway. However, it began the tiny little seed of doubt in the back of my mind that we could ever understand each other. I tucked that away, though, like I had other things in the past and focused on the daily living. Nothing too deep. Nothing too adventurous. Just life. And it was good.

But now, so many years later, I remembered what it had been like to feel like that. To want like that, not material things, but life. I attributed that to my youth and my lack of fulfillment to being an adult. It seemed with adulthood and parenthood, you just did what you were supposed to do to take care of home and bills and family. You lost who you were. I'd barely begun to know myself before I got caught up in being a grown-up. I knew I wanted more.

Church and youth group had been such a huge part of my childhood, I'd tried to incorporate those into my adult life, too. From the beginning, though, Mike and I didn't quite see eye to eye. It wasn't that we didn't want to; we just didn't know how. We came from such different backgrounds.

Once, early in our marriage, we sat outside on the ground, leaning against the side of our house discussing church and religion.

We were not on the same page.

"That doesn't make sense to me, Julie," Mike told me. "Why is it okay to just do anything at all you want to and then say oh, sorry, God, forgive me and then that's okay?"

I sighed. "That's not what I'm saying. You can't just say the words and then that's all okay. You have to really mean it."

He looked at me, skeptical. "How would God know you really mean it?"

"He just knows." I shrugged.

"How?"

"I don't know!" Frustrated, I jumped up and headed toward the door. I didn't know enough to put it in words. Shoot, I didn't even know if I really knew anything at all. I didn't know enough to lead anybody in his faith. Everything deep I'd ever known about God came from David. I listened, David made sense, and I agreed. Even with all that, I didn't quite 'get it' all the way. I continued in my life trying to find it on the outside of me. In my limited knowledge, there was no way I could mentor someone else searching to discover God. I was searching as well. I still had the thought, though, at the back of my mind that even if the God part of it all wasn't real, it didn't matter. As long as we lived 'right' on the outside, then our lives would be good. I didn't realize yet that trying to live from the outside in wasn't truly living.

***

In my youth, I measured my life by the moments with David. The time in between seeing him, I went through all the motions of living. School, work, friends, even dating. Now, however, the time in between was permanent. I hadn't seen him in 12 years and realized I might never again.

My life, rather than being filled with new adventures and excitement as I went through the years, had become full of work and bills and toddlers and babies. I became someone new, not bad, but new and different just the same. I was a wife, a teacher, a mother. I had lost who I was, who I always wanted to be. No longer was I an adventurer. No longer did I feel full of joy and excitement just to wake up and start a day.

Despite being caught up in these routine chores of living, I lay in bed at night wishing for something, some adventure, some excitement. It seemed we spent all our time trying to survive instead of actually living. It's nothing that so many young parents haven't gone through. I just never thought it would happen to me. I knew I should be thankful for all I had, and I was, but I couldn't help but feel a little bitter for missing out on all the excitement I once thought my life would be.

I thought of David and the joy he conveyed always, and I remembered the excitement I felt with him. Joy and excitement like that had to be a choice, right? I'd heard that before - 'happiness is a choice'. I do believe that sometimes it's true. We can definitely choose how to handle some things from the outside. Internally, however, I couldn't make myself be happy. I just didn't understand.

I liked to control things. In that way, I wasn't much different than I'd always been. What I controlled changed as my life evolved, but still I controlled. When anything went not as planned whether it was Mike's behavior, my children's, or anything else, anxiety moved in and it displayed itself through frustration and often anger.

Now, heading out to our old farmhouse, unhappy with our financial woes, unsatisfied with teaching, upset with my inability to know happiness other than just in fleeting moments with my family, I remembered David. I'd been happy with David. Why couldn't I make myself be happy now?

Flowers for the Living

"What do you think of these?" I plopped two books in front of Mike while he tried to look around me to see the TV. Early in the week, I'd picked up the first two books in the *Left Behind* series at the library. Mike told me about them a few years before, but I couldn't think of anything I'd rather do less than read about the Rapture. Until just the past week.

It was late July, hotter than ever, nothing I wanted to do outside, and visiting the library seemed the best option. Besides, in the last week, I hadn't been able to stop thinking about faith. And David. And David's faith. And my own. Thoughts swirled in my brain like a whirlpool. Deeper thoughts than I'd bothered with for many years.

When I stumbled across the *Left Behind* books this time, I felt compelled to read them. Now, I wanted to know Mike's thoughts.

He glanced at the books. "I don't know." He shrugged. "Did you like them?" Mike said the right things but still peeked around me at the characters on the screen.

I took the remote from his hand and turned the TV off. Finally, he looked at me.

"Well, they're literal."

He nodded.

"I don't know if I believe the literal translation of Revelation, but I learned more about what it says." He nodded again. I continued, in conversation with myself for the most part but content with the partial audience he provided.

"I'm restless. I know we go to church, but there has to be more. I've been thinking about my faith and what it means. I just don't know.

"We're always struggling to make ends meet, trying to get along, forcing 'happy' even when we don't feel it. We're so busy trying to make a living and raise our family, I feel like we've forgotten how to make things meaningful. We're doing everything right, so why can't I feel like there's purpose?"

Mike shrugged. "I don't know."

Frustrated, I shook my head at him. "I don't know either. What I really need, I guess, is a book that lays it all out for me. One that tells me exactly who Jesus is and specifically how to incorporate Him into my life."

Mike laughed. "Too bad it's not that easy."

"I know, I know." Thinking about all of it, about faith, brought out passion I hadn't felt in years. "There's this character in the book who talks about how it is faith and not works that leads to eternal life. I know it's hard to believe, but I actually got my bible out and looked up the scriptures about the whole concept of faith versus works. No really, I did." I laughed at Mike then who had slapped his palms on the side of his face in disbelief at the idea of me getting my Bible out.

"It doesn't make sense to me that someone could just say 'I have faith' and not actually do anything. Weren't we called to actually do things in Christ's name. I remember David talking to me on the Tower at Six Flags so long ago. I didn't really understand what he was saying."

Thinking of David made me nostalgic. We'd spoken on the phone a few times through the years, but it had been a while. Our lives had gone in separate directions, as they probably should have I reminded myself frequently.

Despite not having seen him in so long, I never really felt far away from him. He felt like a part of me, a part of who I was. Not being in touch on a daily basis did nothing to change that. As long as he was safe and happy in his world, everything was good. It never occurred to me to think otherwise for him.

I never forgot the thoughts he shared with me so often through the years…about God, about Christ, about living life fully. I had just never understood exactly how to put those thoughts into action or what it really meant to live from the inside out.

"David taught you more than you realize."

I agreed. I'd never kept my friendship with David from Mike. In fact, he'd met him not only at that last party for Kevin but also once before when I took him with David and his youth group to a local amusement park. That was before things became serious with David. Whatever serious might have meant for us.

I'd never shared the depth of our relationship with Mike, or anyone. That part of me was mine. I never felt ashamed of being with David even though I knew it was wrong logically, morally. It never felt wrong though. Loving him never felt wrong to me. It still doesn't. No matter. None of that was relevant to anything presently anyway.

"I wish I could tell him what he meant to me," I whispered. I didn't say the rest of what I was thinking - my only life regret was losing David's friendship. I would have given up all of the last six months of our time together to get him back in my life the way we were. But maybe that never could have happened. Maybe it was too late already before he ever kissed me the first time. I don't know.

"You could tell him," Mike said. "Tell him what he meant to you."

I shook my head. "I couldn't do that."

The last time I'd talked on the phone with David, he'd invited us to come see a Christmas light display. I told him maybe and then didn't go. I just couldn't do it. I couldn't see him.

"Sure you could." Mike sat up then and got excited as he spoke. "I had this college philosophy class where my professor, a part-time minister, taught a concept called 'flowers for the living'. He said rather than wait until a person has passed to send flowers to celebrate his life, send them now while the person can know the impact they have had on your life. The flowers don't have to be literal, of course, but they could be if you wanted. The main thing is to let the person know."

***

A few days later, I returned the *Left Behind* books to the library. Driving home, I thought about faith, about what it means, and about Mike's flowers for the living ideas. David needed flowers. Our last six months would never negate the six previous years and what he meant to me.

I decided to write to him immediately to let him know the impact he had on my life. Despite the physical distance in our lives, I carried him with me throughout my entire adult life. I still considered him the best friend I had ever had.

Call Nothing Thy Own

Monday at work, I searched the Internet for David's email address. Email seemed safer than a phone call. First of all, writing out my thoughts was so much easier for me, and I knew if I spoke to him on the phone I wouldn't end up saying everything I needed him to hear. Besides, last time I'd tried to call him, he'd never called me back.

The December before we moved back to the Midwest, I'd called him on his birthday. It had been a year since the failed Christmas light visit. I left a message…with his wife. It was easy to pass myself off as a former youth member. She was kind and said she'd give him the message. He never called me back.

Only later did I learn they were divorced at that time, or at least separated. Did she give him the message at all? I don't even know. I never have been able to shake the idea that he just didn't want to talk to me. Even now after all we've been through, that idea grips me and refuses to let go. I suppose it's not important anyway and is only a remnant of my insecurities.

A year before, I found a website promoting the musical *Man of La Mancha* David starred in. Yes, I Internet stalked him. That's probably the least of which I might be judged.

At any rate, I remembered that site as I searched for his email and found it again. At first glance, I saw his picture just as I had before. My eyes scanned the page quickly trying to find contact information.

Instead, I saw something else. At the top, in bold, bright font on the dark background, I read, "In Loving Memory of David… "

Underneath, I saw his birthday and then more numbers. Another date. The date he had…died? And then under those dates, a line from the play, "Call nothing thy own except thy soul. Love not what thou art, but only what thou may become."

I stared at the words, not understanding. That end date. He had…died? David died? Only a few weeks previously, during the same time I'd been reading about faith in the Left Behind books and having my discussion with Mike, he'd died?

I knew he'd fought cancer and beaten it. More than once. We'd talked about it. After one of his surgeries to reconstruct his jaw, the doctors used bone from his hip. "Julie," David told me. "Now, I can truly say I have the jawbone of an ass." He'd laughed, and he sounded like the David I'd always known.

It never occurred to me anything bad could really happen to him.

And he'd died.

***

I called Mike; he drove into town and we sat out on the front porch of the building where I taught, and he held me while I cried. David was dead. It made no sense. How could David be dead?

Mike drove me home. I left my car in the parking lot, too devastated to drive. All that time had passed, and I'd never told David what he meant to me. All that time had passed, and I still had never understood fully what he had tried to teach me. What I'd learned from him. As soon as Mike pulled into our driveway, I raced into the house straight to the closet where I pulled out a big tub of things I had collected and kept throughout the years.

I found a book, *Evidence That Demands a Verdict*, David gave me when I graduated from high school and inside that, I found all the letters he had ever written me. I sat on the floor surrounded by his letters and read them one by one. So many of them talked about God, spirituality, and Jesus Christ. David wrote about faith and referred to passages within the book. I looked at it again – it was exactly what I had been looking for, a book explaining exactly who Jesus is. I had that book all along. I never read it. When David gave it to me so many years before, I was most interested in the inscription he wrote on the inside cover of the book. I wasn't interested in the actual contents of the book. I only kept it because it was from David.

Gathering the letters and book in my arms, I clutched them to me and sobbed. If I'd thought I'd lost myself before, now it was true. The best part of me had died.

I'll Never See You Again

Fog surrounded me and showed no signs of lifting. From years of pretending to be who everyone else wanted me to be or who I thought I should be, I found it relatively easy to go through the motions of my life. However, in reality death consumed me. No light or joy filled me.

In every activity, I'd think, "David didn't see that," or (and most commonly), "Who cares? David died."

I couldn't find purpose in anything.

One Thursday evening, I stood in my bedroom, alone in the house for one of those rare times when Mike had taken the kids into town for an activity without me. The house quiet, I could only hear my own breath as I stood over the laundry I'd been folding and stared blankly at the wall in front of me. Thoughts raced through my mind as usual, no beginning and no end, you'redeadyoudieddaviddiedIdon'tunderstanddaviddie dhediedhe'sdead. Over and over.

Out loud I spoke. "I'll never see you again." I tested out the words, listening to the sound of my own voice. By putting them into the air, I was making them tangible. "I'll never see you again." My voice was louder. I heard the panic. Screamed it. Rage. I threw the clothes down I was folding and because that wasn't enough, I bent down, took a shoe off and threw it, too.

Later, still alone, I returned to the website where I'd first learned of David's death. I zoomed in until he filled the screen. I touched his face with my fingertip. Ran my finger across the image of his bottom lip feeling the smooth coolness of the glass, remembering the softness instead, the fullness. Brushing over his cheek, I remember the feel of that scruff, smoothing my palm over it, the bristles tickling me. Rubbing my fingers back and forth through it and him peering at me through half closed eyes, smiling. The memories were too much. I nodded forward resting my forehead against the screen, against his forehead, trying to reach him somehow. Trying to feel him again.

"I don't think I can do this, David," I whispered to him. To no one. There was nobody there. He was gone.

Forever 42

More time passed.

Sitting zombie-like at my computer, I navigated online to a people search site. I typed in David's name and up came his information - name, age, address. He had been a real person living all those years. This people search info. proved it. On the screen, his name was tangible. I could reach out and touch it. I thought about touching him, his hand, his face. About feeling the scruff of his beard rough against my palm. I longed to touch him again, a longing deep throughout me that blanketed any hope or peace that might poke through, and I sat and cried touching his name on the computer screen realizing that I would never see him again.

I looked at his age. 42. That would never change. He would never be 43. Or 44. He would always be 42. At the thought of that, I cried harder, my sobs hitching and gasping. I thought it couldn't get any worse than that.

Weeks later, I visited the same online people search site. This time when I searched his name, nothing came up. I thought maybe I'd mistyped and tried again carefully typing out his name letter by letter. Nothing. He wasn't even 42 any more. He was gone, as if he'd never existed.

I had been wrong before. This was definitely worse.

Rose and Judy

I took too long to grieve and worried that people around me would get tired of me. "Get over it," I told myself. I'd heard that often growing up. My parents raised me with that attitude. Life is tough. Get over it and move on.

I thought something must be wrong with me because, try as I might, I could not get over David's death. A part of me was missing, and I didn't know how to get it back. He was dead. Gone. And it physically hurt me. I never knew grief physically hurt like that – like something had been ripped from me. In a lifetime of never feeling quite good enough, David had filled that role in me. He was my 'goodness'. Without somewhere in the world, how could I ever be good enough again?

People I loved had died before, aunts and uncles, grandparents, and so on. I was sad when those people died. I even wondered about their eternal rest, but I felt comfortable in knowing that they were in Heaven, and I always figured that if Heaven turned out to not exist, it didn't matter anyway because we'd be dead and wouldn't know it. Gruesome? Maybe, but that's how my mind worked.

I equated most of my understanding of myself to David and with him gone, what did that leave for me? Nothing. I simply didn't know. The time had passed to talk about it with my surrounding friends and family. Enough time had passed that I should be over it.

But I wasn't.

Online I found information and comfort through a grief message board where I posted about my grief, about my search for answers about death, about God. Soon after, I received an email from someone named Rose. That first email was guarded – just a few words about how my post had touched her, how she could relate to my grief and all my questions.

Because I desperately needed someone to talk with, I emailed her back immediately. Soon, we became pen pals of sorts. As our email conversations unfolded, we discovered more and more how very alike we were. Her friend, David, had died a day after her birthday from pancreatic cancer the previous summer just as my friend, David, had died two days after my birthday from pancreatic cancer the previous summer. Our grief, our relationships, our thoughts, emotions, feelings…all the same.

Coincidence after coincidence in our situations and lives continued. Rose provided my first ray of hope that perhaps God was somewhere in all of this despair. While Mike was willing to listen some, I wasn't willing to share everything with him, and so his support was limited. Somehow, online, I found someone who really did know my grief.

Also online, I met Judy. Judy's own journey through grief and finding her faith motivated her to reach out and help others going through the same. To Judy, I expressed my fear about questioning God, about doubting His very existence. I grew up learning that we should just have faith, no questions asked. And now, I couldn't do that. I was so very afraid that He would be angry with me for questioning Him. Of course, if He didn't exist, He couldn't get angry. I recognized that but couldn't keep from going in circles with my questions, doubts, fears.

"Julie," Judy wrote to me. "God wants us to question Him. Remember Matthew 7:7, 'Ask and you shall receive, Search and you will find, Knock and the door will be open for you.' It's not only talking about asking for tangible things. Ask for God. Search for Him. He likes it when we question Him because it means we are searching for Him which will only bring us closer to Him."

That resonated with me. For the first time, I understood that it was okay to doubt as long as we didn't mire ourselves in it. Actively doubting, and by that I mean questioning, searching, reading, learning, brought a person closer to God. As long as the search resulted in forward progress, then it was okay.

Along with encouraging emails and Bible study guides sent in the mail, Judy brought to me a new perspective, and I continue to be grateful for her influence on my spiritual growth.

So Angry

The front door slammed behind me as I struggled to balance three bags of groceries plus my school book bags and my purse.

Mike sat on the couch reading to Michael; Zach lay sleeping curled up on the floor in front of the TV.

Kicking aside toy cars and several pairs of little boy shorts, I shuffle stepped across the room making my way into the kitchen, irritated that he didn't get up to help me.

I could see into the kitchen from where I stood and saw the piles of dirty dishes stacked on the counter. That was pretty much the last straw. I snapped.

"What have you done all day?" Irritated. Angry. Tired.

Still without getting up, or even looking up for that matter, he mumbled, "Just hanging with the boys."

I threw the groceries to the ground, spun around, and headed back out the door, slamming it behind me hard enough to rattle the glass.

Yes, I know 'hanging with the boys' was not horrible. In fact, Mike could probably be considered a pretty good guy. I knew he was. Logically.

But my emotions refused to listen to logic. Anger monopolized my feelings frequently, and I took it out on the one most likely to never leave me. Mike. I didn't understand that then, either. It's only in hindsight that I realize.

Then, I only felt rage. It filled me when I was tired, frustrated, sad. I sat on the top porch step, breath hitching, close to a panic attack, trying to suck enough air into my lungs to breathe. When the tears came, whatever blocked my breath opened up and I gasped, sucking in as much air as I could, shoulders heaving, sobbing uncontrollably.

Why couldn't Mike understand? How could David die? No way could I continue the way I was, but I didn't know how to let go of the rage.

(Not) Wearing My Seatbelt

The ch-ch-ch of my tires scratching through puddles hypnotized me. I drove without thinking about the act of driving itself as I wound around Ozark curves and raced up and down Ozark hills. I wondered what would happen if I drove a little faster through the rain, around the curves. My passive aggressive self knew I would never, could never take my own life. Even at the thought of that, I worried what other people might think of me. I thought of my mom killing herself and the despair she left behind. I could never purposely do that. But what if I didn't wear my seatbelt? I wouldn't deliberately wreck, of course, but if I did and had no seatbelt on, well...

I shook my head, purposely snapping myself out of that thought. It was crazy. I didn't want to be crazy.

I would just keep on, alive but not living. Certain my joy and hope was gone forever.

I got home and opened my email. My sweet pen pal Rose had written, "Julie, I know this sounds nuts but sometimes, even though I would never kill myself because of my children, sometimes I consider not wearing my seatbelt and letting whatever happens happen."

My thoughts expressed through Rose. Again. The similarities we shared in our experiences, our emotions, and our thoughts continued to amaze me. Without knowing what she was doing with her own confession, Rose comforted me. A coincidence like that could only come from God. In one of my most desperate times, God reminded me I wasn't alone.

My despair could so easily have concealed this provision. I recognized and felt grateful for this tiny moment of grace.

Asking for Signs

In my first steps towards turning to God, I began to pray. Every night.

My early prayers sounded like this - "Please God. I'm not sure if I'm supposed to ask for this, but please send me a sign that I'll know that David knows how much I cared."

And then, too, "Please God. I don't know how I can continue. What do I have to offer? What do I have to give? All that I am was because of David, and now he's dead. I don't understand."

I couldn't say specifically what I didn't understand. Really, I didn't understand anything at all – David dying, what it meant. If David could die, then what was the point in anything? I could see no point. I wasn't sure of my purpose before, and now I doubted any purpose at all.

Despite my doubts and my fear that the whole God thing was a farce, I continued to cling to Him. Some sort of belief must have still been within me. I'm afraid to think of what might have happened had that not been there. I prayed, and then I prayed some more.

One day, I drove home from work, praying again. I prayed all the time. I knew I needed help, but I didn't know how to go about getting it. "Please, God. Please give me a sign that everything is okay."

A feeling of peace that I can't really explain washed over me for a brief second. I glanced over and saw through the trees a huge sign. Only part of it peeked out between the branches, but that one part was enough for me. In large cursive letters, I read 'David'. The timing of the sign right after my prayer wasn't completely lost on me. I wondered if that was my sign. What is a sign anyway? A coincidence? Maybe. Of course, David was on my mind. Maybe that's why I'd only just noticed this literal sign that had been there all along.

I reached over and flipped on the radio. George Michael was singing, "You gotta have faith, faith, faith." Definitely not a religious song, but what timing! Faith. I laughed and drove on home. I told Mike right away.

"I think you got your sign, Julie," he told me. "Everything is okay."

Hmm. I liked the thought of that, but it wasn't enough. How could I be sure? How could I be positive that God sent me a sign and that it wasn't coincidence? I didn't know. I wanted David to be okay so badly. I wanted God to be a part of everything so much. I feared reading something into it to make myself feel better. It became critical I find out for sure.

A few days later, Mike emailed me at work saying he was on his way into town; he had something to give me. His email was short and abrupt. What in the world?

I waited outside for him. He arrived, a shaken look on his face, carrying something with him.

I took his arm and led him to the porch bench where we sat together.

"I was cleaning the basement," he said. "I decided to get rid of some of those old mildewed boxes." Our house was old, the basement a mess. The mildewed boxes had long needed to be cleaned out.

He continued, "I was about to haul one of the boxes out to burn, and I decided instead to look through it first. As I dug through it, I found this." He held out a cassette tape. When I saw it, my jaw dropped. George Michael's *Faith*. Let me tell you, we never listened to George Michael. Mike bought it for a friend years before and somehow had never given it away. We threw out most of our cassettes years before as we made the transition to CDs.

"I thought you'd get a kick out of me finding this tape after your 'gotta have faith' sign, so I tossed it back into the box to carry out later rather than now. I headed upstairs but decided to go back and get it to make sure nothing happened to it. I dug through the box again to find it, but it had shifted down underneath papers and junk. Finally, I found it again. Right on top of this."

I looked at what he held out to me. Another cassette. I recognized David's handwriting on the cover. Like with the *Faith* cassette, no mildew covered this one, a cassette of David speaking at a retreat years before, speaking about faith and living fully.

I just looked at Mike, amazed at the magnitude of all of these coincidences.

"I know." Mike nodded at me, understanding what I felt at that very moment. "I grabbed both tapes and ran up the stairs. Halfway up, such emotion overcame me. Such presence. I literally fell to my knees and thanked God. I promised Him I'd make sure you got this. I felt David, Julie. There's no other explanation. It felt like David. I don't know. I don't know."

I reached for the cassette. Running my fingers over David's name written by his own hand, I thought about my 'signs'. What was I supposed to learn from them? Faith. I knew that much. Coincidences or not, faith in God was key. "Thank you, Lord," I prayed silently. "If these things are really from you, please send me another sign so that I can know for sure."

The fear of being wrong kept me from allowing God to truly comfort and reassure me. I worried about asking for so many signs. I feared God would get impatient with me. I felt so lost and lonely and couldn't see the good right in front of me – my husband, my kids, my extended family, my friends. I just didn't know how to be me without David.

I often read the story of Gideon. The Lord told Gideon He would be with him. Gideon, though, wasn't sure if he should believe. "If now I have found favor in your eyes, give me a sign that it is really you talking to me," he asked. (Judges 6:17) The Lord gave him the signs he asked for and then Gideon, in his continuous insecurity said, and I'm loosely paraphrasing now, "Don't be mad at me but please let me make one more request."

The comfort I found in Gideon's story was not only that he kept asking for signs as I was doing but that the Lord didn't get impatient with Gideon. The Lord just kept providing signs. That gave me hope that He also would have patience with me.

Hearing God

Grief has no distinct stages. Not really. I'd make progress and think I understood God and purpose, life and love one day, and then the next fear immobilized me.

One day, I lay in my bed curled up in a ball. My family watched T.V. in the next room, but I only wanted to be alone. I wasn't crying; instead, I prayed – frantically. As fast as I could think the words, I prayed them – desperately.

"God, I don't know what to do. Why does it hurt so much? How can David be dead? What does that mean? Help me. Please. Please help it not hurt. I don't think I can go on. Nothing makes sense. If we just die, then what's the point in anything? Please help me not hurt. I don't know what to..."

"Listen." Something interrupted me – another thought – not really a voice. A thought interrupting my frantic prayer. In my head I heard it. The force of the word caused me to pause. "Listen." I 'heard' again. Lying very still, I stopped praying and waited to see if anything else came. When nothing did, I still didn't go back to my prayer. Instead, I considered "Listen". Realization struck. In prayer, I must not only ramble my requests, but I must stop and listen to what God has to say to me. My answers may not come in the form of tangible events; they might instead come as feelings of peace and support…with knowing that He is real, and that I'm not alone. That in itself provides strength when nothing else can.

Listen. Maybe I interrupted myself to give this advice, but I don't think so. In my anguish, it never would occur to me stop my plea and tell myself to listen. Somehow God had gotten through to me even though I wasn't being still.

I remembered sitting on the couch with David at camp, focused only on how the hairs on his thighs curled up around the edge of his shorts and how much I wanted to touch him, and him asking me if I listened to God.

I'd never known what he meant. Only now did I understand that to hear, I must first be still and quiet.

Unsure

Many months into my grief, I dreamed this:

I gaze across rolling hills and feel a peace unlike any I'd ever imagined. I can see so clearly; colors shine brightly and details stand out vividly. Even blades of grass are distinctly individual as they gently bow to me in the breeze.

On the left, a field of flowers dots the landscape with color. I'm unfamiliar with what kind of flowers they might be, but their beauty takes my breath away. To my right, a lake with waves gently lapping up onto a sandy shore catches my eye. I see a lone rowboat out in the middle, a man fishing.

I think it's David.

It must be David.

Crying out to him, my words catch silently in the shimmer of the sky, I desperately work to get his attention, but he can't hear me. I fear the thought of him being so close but unreachable.

I'm hoping to find the days when the fears don't come. The tears don't come. I look for him in the mist of the evening. Falling gently, over the water. Hanging there, ready for the final fall.

I wake up and feel so alone.

Understanding Love

I stretched out across our living room floor, the kids playing around me. Every so often one of the boys' toy cars would bump into me, but I didn't move. Instead, I just waited for whichever kid it was to get it off me, and I would sink back into my own thoughts.

Death made no sense to me. What in the world was the point of living if you were just going to die? I thought of David and how full of life he was. Remembering the joy that radiated from him, I couldn't even begin to fathom that it was gone. Dead. I thought about watching his hands fly over a piano keyboard or strum his guitar; I remembered riding roller coasters and cruising around in his old orange pickup truck and endless conversations about all that was happening in the world. I remembered the way he looked at me, like what I had to say mattered and how he challenged me to embrace life and to learn and grow and be confident in myself. And what did it matter now? David was dead.

I thought about what remained of him. Of his possessions. His family. He took none of that with him. Nothing. So what did he take? And what did he leave behind? I loved David, it was true. I had loved him from almost the very first time I'd seen him up on that rock fireplace mantel playing his guitar for a crowd of adoring kids. He was the best friend I had ever had. And David loved, too…he loved his family, he loved Jesus, he loved living, and he loved me. His love, that's what he gave the world. And that's what he took with him. All the love that had been given him. I realized in that moment that only love transcends 'here' and 'there'. Life was not merely about existing; it was about loving and living in love.

I hadn't yet put it together that God is love. I'd heard that before, of course, a million times. But it had always been an expression and not inclusive of all love. I guess I thought there was God's love and then just love, love. I don't know. I hadn't figured it out yet. But understanding the importance of love being the foundation of everything guided me in the right direction. It suddenly made sense that our lives should be made up of every effort to feel that love and also, more importantly, to share it.

Giving it to God

As teenagers, my cousin and I were very close. She knew what David meant to me, so I wrote her pouring out my grief, my doubt in God, my fears. She wrote back to me, "Julie, I wish I had the words to help you. All I really know, though, is that when I have something like this that is so big there is really nothing else to do except give it to God."

Give it to God. I understood what she meant. I wanted to give it to God; I just didn't know how. I kept looking outside of me for God so that I could give it to Him. I even asked a few times, "How can I give this to you, God?" Nothing worked. I either didn't know how to give it to Him or He wasn't willing to take it.

We still lived in the old farmhouse. The inside, a strange layout, consisted of open rooms and open doorways with no actual doors in them. In fact, the only door inside the entire house belonged to the one bathroom. Fortunately, it had a lock on it. I frequently took refuge there in my grief because I didn't want Mike and the kids to see me so sad. I would put on a happy face as best I could and then would lock myself in the bathroom for sometimes hours at a time sobbing in the bathtub or sitting on the side of it staring blankly at the tile wall.

One day, I locked myself in. I put the lid to the toilet down and sat talking to David, talking to God, sobbing uncontrollably. I was at a loss. I didn't see how I could go on any more. There seemed to be no point in living. If David could die, David who was full of life and joy and love and fun, then what was the point? I could find no point in anything. I cried even harder. Rock bottom. I've heard that expression and in looking back at me on that day, I know that's where I had fallen. I hit rock bottom. There was no where else to go.

"God!" I cried out. "God, I don't know what to do. I'm so lost. I'm so lost. I give this to you!"

I sat for a moment still crying. In my anguish, I poured everything out, everything that I had been, everything I had become. No longer could I handle anything at all by myself. I no longer possessed the ability to control my feelings and stop grieving. There was no more pretense. With that deluge of emotion, I felt something new inside of me. Tiny, down deep within me, I felt it. Just a little. Hope. Peace. A minute niggling that seemed to assure me that everything would be okay. I would be okay.

In a storybook, everything would be perfect from that moment on. In my reality, things were still difficult. That little piece of hope, though, allowed me to move forward. It gave me something to hang on to in my deepest despair.

Understanding

The last of my after lunch homeroom students had filed out of the classroom on their way to 6th hour. Since my plan time followed, no new kids came in to take their places.

On automatic pilot, I stepped through the rows, straightening each desk, putting them in order. I needed order to hold on to.

I took a deep breath and leaned against my own desk, relishing the quiet that came after the busy-ness of thirty 12 year-olds in a single room. It took all of my energy to 'perform' for my students. Performing was all it was. Doing a good job was instilled in me from early childhood and so I knew how to make everything look good – to make it appear right. On the inside, though, I still felt blah. Dead. No feeling. Nothing made sense to me. No purpose mattered. The peace I felt in the bathroom when I first gave my grief to God had been so tiny, it was easy for me to ignore.

Tears came and as much as I tried to stop them from spilling, they ran down my cheeks faster than I could wipe them away.

"God!" I cried out in a desperate whisper not wanting to be heard by any of my co-workers. "God, I don't understand. How can David be dead? How can someone so big, so full of life be dead. David was the one we all waited for. He was the one we wanted. When he entered the room it was like someone turned all the lights on and we could finally get started with whatever it was we wanted to do."

None of it made any sense. I continued, "Lord, I don't understand how that light can be gone. How can there ever be any light again?"

My heart was raw. Open. Desperate for an answer.

And then I felt it...fullness, peace, love. Inside of me. This time, I sighed in relief, and I thought these words that I know came from God: "It's in you. The light is in you."

I knew from that moment what it all meant. David's greatness came not from himself but from God.

David allowed God to live through him. My dear sweet friend wasn't the light; God was. And God was available for me, too. I might not shine in the same way David did – I don't sing well, I'm not that funny, my personality isn't quite that big, but still I could let God live and breathe and…shine through me in a way that fits for me. I can be kind. Patient. I can care. I can talk about God and what He has done for me – not 'outside' of me but on the inside. I spent so much time asking for signs, looking outside of me for peace. God was kind and patient; He provided what I asked for, and He let me work through my grief and create my own relationship with Him. He was steady and firm and lovingly waited for me to come to Him. He filled me with His spirit and taught me how to truly be alive. From the inside…where it comes with the knowledge that no matter what is happening on the outside, it will all be okay.

For the first time, I truly felt like I could live.

PART FOUR: Prove It (He Still Exists)

Desperate to Know, Scared to Be Wrong

It's difficult to describe the urgency I felt trying to find David, to reach him, to knowforsurewithoutadoubt that he still existed, that he knew how I felt about him, and that I find out how and what I had ever meant to him. As the sharpest pains of grief subsided, I did feel that he still existed. Somehow.

I'd lost a part of me. The one person who had filled me and made me feel like I could do anything was gone. Despite the fact I hadn't seen him in 12 years, just knowing that he lived somewhere and loved somewhere happily had always been enough to keep me going. With him dead, though…

My life became a combination of living here and completing all necessary tasks and trying to find there where David might be. I would say it was a balance, but that would only be wishful thinking on my part. There was no balance. I spent so much time searching. My family wasn't neglected, don't get me wrong. In fact, having discovered that unconditional love flowing through me I had become, for the most part, more patient and more accepting with Mike and with my children. Not that I didn't occasionally lose it. However, I spent hours writing David letters, pouring out my thoughts, asking for answers. In the evenings, once I'd attended to the physical needs of my family (with much help from Mike who seldom wavered), I read everything I could get my hands on about life after death. I read religious books, spiritual books, new age. I read about reincarnation and mediums. About what heaven looks like. If it had to do with death and an afterlife, I read it. I also spent hours most days searching online. I found chat rooms devoted to grief and to after death communication. I learned everything I could. Along the way, I would desperately ask David, "Are you still alive? Do you exist?" and then I would add, "Prove it. Please!"

What made everything so extraordinary was not just what happened but the timing in which it happened. Something would happen to me that I thought might be a sign from God or communication from David, and then within the next day or two I would read about or hear in a chatroom about that very type of communication or information when I'd had no idea before what it might mean or that it was not uncommon from spirit. My Christian church background, albeit a liberal one, hadn't prepared me for many spiritual things.

From dreams, to visions, to sensing presence, to all of the signs and coincidences - I finally learned to quit questioning, start accepting, and just say thank you. It took a very long time and didn't happen all in a neat little series of events. But it did happen, and I finally accepted it all. Eventually. What I write about in this section only covers some of the communications I (and others) received from David. While there were many more, these are some of my favorites and are the ones I could not rationalize away.

I Want to Be with You

I began to feel David's presence. Out of the blue, something would come over me, I can't really describe it, but I would do more than think about him. It was like I could feel his energy. It would start with pressure in my lower belly and then move upward into my chest. And then I'd just know.

For many months, even through years off and on, I questioned and worried my grief had consumed me so deeply that I made up the feeling of him. Could my memories be so strong that somehow they caused my brain and body to feel him? Can memories do that? Probably. But this seemed more. I doubted but also hoped enough that I began to talk to him, not just in the desperate prayers for him to be okay but also in every day acknowledgment that he was present.

Crazy? Maybe. I worried about that, too.

The vague and abstract nature of thoughts and emotions kept me skeptical for years. I needed tangible. I wanted to 'see'.

Dreams gave me that option, and I learned after time to tell the difference between random dreams and actual visits from David. Although I'd heard of them before, actual spirit visits in dreams were a new concept to me; however, just like with other spiritual happenings, I experienced new things first and then later found out there were actual names for those phenomena.

Just a few weeks after he died, I dreamed this:

Frantically, I searched for David. I looked everywhere - in crowds, in stores, in my house. I couldn't find him; desperate and sobbing, I kept searching. I saw everything in vivid clear color, sharp images. I hadn't realized yet it was a dream.

Somehow, I ended up in my grandmother's house. As I walked through her kitchen, I recognized finally that I was in a dream. My grandmother passed years before. I haven't been to her house since. I kept crying, wandering through the house, looking for David. I glanced up at the doorway leading into the dining room and noticed a man leaning against the frame. I didn't recognize him until he turned towards me. It was David.

"Remember me?" he smiled. I knew that smile.

I fell towards him trying to reach him as quickly as I could. He wrapped his arms around me, and I held onto him laying my head on his chest, sobbing almost uncontrollably.

"I want to be with you. I want to be with you," I repeated, although I didn't really say the words out loud. They were in my head; I thought them to him.

He didn't answer but just held me while I cried.

The front of his olive green dress shirt was soaked with my tears and from my running nose. Gross.

"Oh my gosh, I'm sorry. I'm snotting all over your shirt," I said through my tears. I felt bad about ruining it. It was a nice shirt.

"It doesn't matter," he said, holding me tighter. I felt in his answer his amusement with me. So real. A memory or something new?

"David, I want to be with you."

He still had no answer for that.

I wanted him to say something, to reassure me that we could be together. My brain took over, and I began rationalizing. "I don't mean I want to be with you right now. I don't mean I'm going to kill myself or anything. I just mean, you know, eventually. Forever. I want to be with you. I know I'm with Mike now here and that's okay and I want that to be okay and good and I will…"

I rambled on, and as I did I found myself apart from David, across the room. His image faded. I tried to get back to him, but I couldn't. I thought he was pulling away from me. Maybe I rambled too much. Maybe he was saying we couldn't be together. I didn't know.

Then, still dreaming, I 'woke up' on a mattress in a side room off the dining room of my grandmother's house. When I woke up in the dream, I understood I had been dreaming. Immediately, I woke up for real. I lay in my bed and worried and wondered why he had pulled away from me. It wasn't until much later that I realized it was just as likely I had pulled away from him as my brain began to worry and think about physical world things. I don't know. Maybe.

My Son Saw an Angel

I pulled up to the curb of my brother and sister-in-law's house, in a hurry as usual. I was late to pick up my daughter from daycare. My son, 7 years old, sat behind me in the middle seat. I left him there as I raced in to grab a book I planned to borrow for my weekly book study. As I settled back into the van, I tossed the book on the front passenger seat and started to put the van in drive. My son announced loudly, "Hey, Mom, this reminds me of the time I saw the angel."

What? I hadn't heard of any time he'd seen an angel. I had no idea what he was talking about.

"What angel?" I asked him.

"Remember, I saw an angel." I could see his face in my rear view mirror, eyebrows raised but face very serious.

I thought carefully. No, I'm sure I'd remember an angel sighting. "I don't think you told me about that, son." I peered back at him in the mirror again and watched him scrunch his face up in thought.

"Well," he said, "I know I told Daddy."

"Will you tell me now?"

"Sure!" His little face lit up and he wiggled himself up taller in his booster seat. "It was that time right after school started. You had to come pick up Sissy from Aunt Helen's. I was sitting here waiting for you and looking out the window, and I saw an angel walking toward the van."

"What did she look like?" I interrupted him. I wasn't sure what to think at this point. He was my imaginative child. I felt pretty sure he just thought he saw something.

"It was a he, Mom. He was really tall and had dark hair and a really big smile. His eyes were super blue and he had on a blue shirt and blue jeans and black shoes. There was light spread allll around him in a million different directions."

My breath caught. He described David, at least in general – tall, dark hair, big smile, blue eyes. My son had never seen David, not even a picture of him. I never discussed him. Not in my adult life. I'd set him aside so that I could live my life without him. Not that I didn't think about him frequently, but I never talked about him to or in front of my kids. Not even in the past few months since he died. I'm sure they may have noticed I'd been upset or at least 'different', but I felt pretty positive I hadn't mentioned his name around them much less what he looked like.

I tried not to react or to lead him in any way. As casually as I could, I asked him, "What happened next?"

My son, still sitting up tall and wiggling around in his seat excitedly, answered, "He walked closer to the van smiling the whole time, and then when he got close, the light folded all around him and covered him up and then it got smaller and smaller until it disappeared."

Still contemplating whether or not he could have made up the story or at the least, heard a description of David or heard me talking about him, I asked him one more question. "How did it make you feel when you saw him walking toward you?" I figured if he were making it up, I'd hear how scary it was or how nervous it made him…like he might portray it as a spooky story.

"It made me feel good, Mama," he answered, his voice light and cheerful. "I felt happy all over kind of like when I get to go to Going Bananas." Going Bananas was a local indoor play place with bouncy houses and roller skating, etc. He definitely was happy whenever he got to go to there.

***

Later that night, I approached my son about the angel again. I'd thought about it all day, discussing it with Mike and running over it again and again in my mind. In my constant quest to not be wrong about anything, I overanalyzed, attempting to find a logical answer to my son's sighting/story. I couldn't seem to discredit him, and so I decided to check one more thing.

I held out a picture of David to him. It was one of only a few I had; I'd found it tucked away in an old photo album stored in a back closet. After I learned of his death, I'd dug out the tub that held all those memories and gone through them over and over. I felt confident, though, that none of my children had seen them.

"Do you know who this is," I asked my sweet son.

He looked up at me from the little plastic cars he was playing with, paused only for about half a second and said, "Sure, Mom. That's the angel." Without missing a beat, he went back to his cars. Obviously to him, it was no big deal. To me, wow.

It was still early in my grieving process, and I wasn't quite ready to completely accept what my son saw yet. I'm not sure if it was because if I accepted him seeing David as an angel that meant I had to accept that David was dead or if it was because I was so afraid of being made a fool of by believing something sooo crazy.

Now, I know.

There are a variety of beliefs about what angels are: if angels really exist, if they are celestial beings which have never incarnated, if they are our loved ones passed. To my seven-year-old, he had no other word but angel. He believed. I believe.

I Never Realized

I began keeping a dream journal as the visions that played through my head while I slept became even more vivid than usual. I've always been a dreamer, but now, even when David didn't appear in my dreams I knew the themes and messages I received were important. Over time I came to find recurring themes and learned things I never knew.

I entered through a door into darkness. I sensed someone walking towards me, but I saw nothing at all. As the presence approached, I knew it was David; I could feel him, his energy. He held out his hands. I reached for him and listened closely because he'd begun to speak. I knew that whatever he said was important and that I must remember it.

"I never realized that I never told you how I felt. I didn't think about that. I always thought it was kind of like, you know, have money will travel. I wasn't here long, though, before I knew the truth."

I repeated his words over and over. By the fourth time, he dropped my hands, and I felt him move away. I repeated them one more time and then woke up.

Because of how deeply the dream affected me, I wrote about it to a group of dream interpreters at an online message board searching for meaning and for validation that a dream might possibly be real.

"It sounds like he was talking about his life review," one of them responded. "When he says he wasn't there long before he knew the truth, he must be talking about finding understanding of his actions while he was still here."

I'd never heard of a life review, but I agreed that's what it sounded like, that he'd learned something after he died.

What could I take from that? That without me knowing anything about a life review, I'd dreamed of one. That's an answer in itself. Also, if David had learned something new after he died, that meant that somehow he still lived. He still existed.

I liked that thought.

Tigger and More

My daughter, Rachel, stood in my sister's kitchen smack dab in the middle of the floor. Megan put groceries away in a nearby cabinet while I propped myself up in the doorway looking in.

"What are you doing, Sis?" I asked Rachel as she'd begun to twirl 'round and 'round. She didn't answer. At just turned two years old, she frequently didn't answer when she got caught up in something.

Faster she spun, and then...

"Wonderful thing about Tiggers. Tiggers are wonderful things..." she began singing in a two-year-old voice with two-year-old pronunciation, but her words were unmistakable.

She continued. "'Ouncy, 'ouncy, 'ouncy, 'ouncy, fun, fun, fun, fun, fun." Spinning the whole time.

I stared.

I knew for a fact I'd never shown her any Winnie the Pooh or Tigger and her sitter had no TV at all and yet she danced and sang to a song David used to sing to my three-year-old niece almost 20 years before.

"Rachel, where did you learn that song?" I had to say it several times as she still wasn't listening.

Still, she didn't answer me. Instead she giggled. And then giggled some more. "Again, David." Rachel shouted out, still giggling. "Again," she cried joyfully, "David, again."

***

I dragged myself into the kitchen and headed straight for the coffee pot. Mike stood at the stove frying bacon. The smell caused my stomach to rumble.

Pouring coffee I clutched my mug and leaned back against the counter, watching Mike cook. His hair stuck up in all directions. I grinned noticing that and also his rumpled shirt and flannel sleep pants. I felt such appreciation for him rolling right out of bed and coming in to cook for us. Typically, he slept late; we didn't even have anywhere to be on that Saturday, so it surprised me to see him.

Little footsteps pat-patted onto the tile kitchen floor, and I glanced over to see 2 1/2 year old Rachel come in. Still in her pjs, she carried her pink and yellow striped baby blanket. She was so cute.

Smiling, she waved at Mike. "Hi, Daddy," she called out, still waving. Then, before either of us could say anything she pointedly looked to the right of where Mike stood, waved again to seemingly nobody and cheerfully called out, "Hi, David." She then ran to her high chair to climb up for breakfast and left us staring at each other eyebrows raised.

***

I heard giggling and talking in the kitchen, and then a loud thunk as something hard hit the floor. Then, giggles again. I knew it had to be Rachel, but I couldn't imagine what she was doing. She was laughing too hard for me to understand her words.

I tiptoed to the door and peeked in. Around and around she spun, giggling so hard tears squeezed from the corners of her eyes.

"Look at me," she cried out happily. "Look at me, David. David, look at me." And then she'd fall on the floor in a heap crumpled over in helpless laughter before she'd get up and do it again.

***

Rachel became an almost daily source of communication from David. Or at least, acknowledgment he was around. I could picture him whispering to her, "Rachel, Rachel…they can't hear me, so you talk to me. That way they'll know."

Even though I couldn't hear him, I began talking to him all the time.

"David, I don't think Rachel ever heard us mention your name, but if she did it would have only been your first name. Tell her your last name. Get her to say that. That way I'll know it's really you."

Within two days, my sweet tiny toddler ran circles around the living room saying David's last name over and over again. I could only shake my head. Disbelief.

But…belief, too. Hope. The promise of what this meant swelled in my upper abdomen and heart as air in a balloon filling me so full of spirit, of joy, of love, and of peace I thought I might burst. There didn't seem any way to contain that feeling, and it helped me to understand early on that this feeling was not meant to stay trapped inside of me. Purpose could be found in it, in letting it out into the world. There was no way I could contain it once I allowed it to take over.

Overwhelmed by emotion, I tamped it down, ignored it, and promptly fell back into despair. Finding that middle ground of allowing that love to lead me without letting the despair of not having David there and not trusting in God and that it was all real made the day-to-day very hard.

Don't Doubt David

Because I'd grown up with Jesus as my 'spirit guide', I never knew about the idea that we all have spirit guides. And then I dreamed about one of mine.

I sat facing a lady I did not recognize; she wore a bright red shirt and looked to be in her mid-thirties with long straight soft dark hair and a dark complexion.

"I don't know you." Conversation in my dreams typically comes through my thoughts.

She smiled. "Don't look at me with your eyes. Feel who I am."

"Laura?"

She nodded.

"I do know you."

She nodded again.

"How?"

She shrugged. "It's not important. Tell me about your grief."

Dream time doesn't seem the same as awake time. I felt we talked for a very long time, all of our words continuing to come through thoughts and feelings rather than being spoken.

All of a sudden, Laura looked directly into my eyes and spoke very clearly to me. "Don't doubt David," she said. "He loved you so very much."

Maddie Sees Him

"Can you please come out and help me walk Maddie to class?"

I looked up from the papers I had been grading to see Taylor, one of my 7th grade students at my classroom door. Smiling, I stood up. "Sure, Taylor."

Maddie was one of our developmentally challenged students. She came to my class every day as I taught an elective available to all students. She was a nice girl who was known to occasionally have a stubborn streak. She frequently talked to imaginary friends. Other students were used to her and typically helpful. Taylor had taken on the task of making sure Maddie made it in the door after recess, down the long hallway, and to her classroom safely. Because the hallway was filled with other students, Maddie frequently became overwhelmed and refused to walk. I recently had begun helping Taylor when she needed, talking to Maddie with her, waiting out the crowd, and getting Maddie to her classroom.

That day was no different. I stepped out in the hall and saw Maddie at the other end near the exit doors standing stock still in the middle of the hall. She seemed to be talking to herself or to one of her imaginary friends. It occurred to me then, watching her, that I'd read stories with the philosophy that those with developmental challenges could see spirit just as it was thought that children could. I already believed children could; my children had. Could all of those imaginary friends Maddie talked to be spirits?

Just as always, I helped Taylor with Maddie, and we got her up the hall, past my room which was at the far end, and to her classroom. Later that night, I thought more about the possibility of Maddie seeing spirit.

I talked to David about it. "David," I said out loud, not really knowing if he was there, if he cared, or if I was just nuts talking out loud to nobody. "David," I continued. "If it's true Maddie is seeing spirit and not just talking to imaginary people, show yourself to her. Talk to Maddie. Let me see it and know it. Please."

Foolish or not, I was curious. It was just one of the many 'tests' I gave David. Sweet, patient David, right? Thank goodness he is.

Two days later Taylor stepped into my classroom.

"Having trouble getting Maddie up the hallway again?" I asked her.

"No, it's not that. Well, kind of. I thought we were having a good day. She walked all the way up here until right outside of your room. She refuses to go past your room," Taylor told me.

I jumped up to help and walked out into the hall. Maddie stood directly outside my doorway, bent forward at the waist. Her left hand was on her hip and her right raised as she shook her finger at someone (no one) in front her. Whoever it was, she was letting him have it.

I intended to interrupt her and encourage her to move along faster. Then, I heard what she was saying.

"David! David, move out of my way!" she spoke sternly as if she was reprimanding someone. As soon as I heard the name David, I stopped abruptly. Was it a coincidence her imaginary friend on that day was named David? I listened and watched her keep shaking her finger at the air.

"Now, David. You have to move out of my way. I have to go to class." She continued on with similar commands, really letting him have it. She glanced over and saw me and paused. I stepped forward. "Who are you talking to, Maddie?" I asked her.

"David. He won't let me get by."

I looked into the empty space in front of her. "Hi, David," I said to no one. "Will you let Maddie by now so she can go to class?" Taylor stood with us watching the whole incident, but she stayed very quiet. I turned to Maddie. "Is he going to let you by now."

Maddie looked up, smiled, and nodded. "Thanks, David," she said. Without another word, she lurched forward towards her classroom. She never mentioned David again.

Finally Playing His Guitar for Me

From online friends, I learned of Ocallah, a medium known for her compassion, knowledge, and most of all, her accuracy with details. Desperate to know David still existed, that he knew how I felt, and that I wasn't making up all that was happening, compelled me to make an appointment. Here are transcripts of a few of my favorite parts:

Ocallah: I'm getting a male figure to your side.
Me: Okay.
Ocallah: is he a teacher...or are you? Something about working with kids.
Me: Yes.
Ocallah: I feel he liked to share what he knew, like a mentor.
Me: Yes.
Ocallah: Oh my god, this is your husband.
Me: No, not my husband.
Ocallah: He connects emotionally like a husband.
Me: Yes, I understand that.
Ocallah: He has a playful energy. Kind of like a big kid.
Me: Yes, definitely.
Ocallah: He has to be your husband. He's calling you his best friend. The emotional connection like this. So many layers – friend, husband, partner.
Me: (crying) I understand.
Ocallah: Did he have cancer or aids, leukemia...something that ran all through.
Me: Yes, cancer.

Ocallah: Did he grow a beard?

Me: Yes. (God! I loved when he grew his beard!)

Ocallah: He wants you to know he's playing the guitar for you…and singing.

Me: Yes!

***

Ocallah: You guys had an interesting relationship, according to him.

Me: Yeah.

Ocallah: It's like, forbidden fruit.

Me: That's right.

Ocallah: But he really loves you, like seriously loves you. It's this passionate love, and it's also very unconditional. You know, it's like, I would feel so compelled towards that. I would want to be with him. So I'm sure that's what you struggled with; I want to be with you.

***

Ocallah: He seems funny to me. He must have had a good sense of humor.

Me: Yes, definitely.

Ocallah: Was he French?

Me: No.

Ocallah: Who's Phil? Or Phillip? Or…Philippe?

Me: (laughing) I dated someone from France named Philippe. He used to tease me about him.

Ocallah: I think he still is.

Not quite two months after David had promised to get his guitar out and play for me again came the day in the truck when I told him I couldn't see him anymore. In that time, he never had brought his guitar. It never occurred to me I wouldn't hear him play his guitar again. Or that I'd never see him again at all (not counting that brief moment at Kevin's welcome home party). But somehow, he found a way to keep his promise.

I love that.

White Rabbits Everywhere

Hoping to help my sister, I wrote a letter to our mother.

Dear Mom,

Megan decided to have a reading. I know she wants you and Grandma to come through. I don't really remember you much so I don't know what to ask for for Megan, but please say something that she'll know it's definitely you. Maybe you could come through with a bunny…a white bunny…

While I have no memories of our mother since she died before my first birthday, I based my request to her on a photo we have of her standing on the curb in front of our house holding a white rabbit. From the stories I've heard about her, she had a sweet and nurturing nature. She loved animals and adopted every stray she found.

Megan's reading came and went and while the medium hit on many specific details and our grandmother came through, nothing was said about Mom or about a white rabbit.

The next week I called for my own reading. Three-quarters of the way through, the reading took a turn away from David.

"I don't know if this is for you or your sister."

I waited, curious about what might come next but also not wanting her to get away from David. I needed more validation he was there, or here…that he was okay.

"There's something," she paused briefly. "Something about a bunny. A white bunny. Is that for you or your sister?"

Speechless, I sat. I hadn't even told Megan about the letter I'd written Mom about the bunny. "It's for both of us," I finally squeaked out. I couldn't wait to tell everybody what had just happened.

***

I sat at my computer staring at the chat window. Online chat groups kept me connected to David in the only way I knew how to stay connected with him. Whether there were readings or not, I could talk about him there. Without worrying about bothering people too much, I was able to continue talking about my grief. Typing out my thoughts and feelings helped me process all I felt. And there was a bunch.

"David?" I spoke out loud hoping (pretending?) he could hear me. "David, are you here? Where are you? I miss you."

To the left of my computer sat a framed picture of the two of us together. I stared at it for a minute and then 'click' something in my brain shifted, and I noticed the shirt I was wearing in the picture. Music notes surrounded two white bunnies dancing together.

White bunnies?

"David, what does that mean? I thought the bunnies were about my mom and for Megan. Were they about this shirt? What does it mean? How are they connected?"

I couldn't wrap my head around two significant events involving white rabbits. "Is it you?" I asked him. "Or is it my mom?"

A thought occurred to me. "Maybe it's both. It's not specifically about David. Not about my mom. It's about connectedness. We're all spirit. All connected. All together. Maybe that's my lesson. Is that it?"

I sat quietly but didn't hear an answer.

***

I wiped my eyes one more time and climbed back into the van. Mike and the kids had driven around the cemetery until I'd signaled for them to come back and pick me up from David's grave.

While I'd been feeling him, questioning, experiencing his spirit for some time, only recently had I begun to accept it all as real. How could so many coincidences continue to occur? Sure, I could be nuts, but I didn't think so. Not usually.

Away from his grave, I recognized his spirit, felt his personality, believed the signs and symbols he sent assuring me he still existed. Sitting at his headstone, all that comfort was lost. The thought of the body I'd loved so much in the ground was more than I could bear and the reality of the space where it would be forever crashed into me. It squeezed my heart, lungs, and stomach in a vise. And yet, I couldn't stay away.

"Tell me it's okay. Please. Tell me it's okay." I pleaded to him as I'd sat cross-legged in front of his engraved name.

I felt nothing sitting there except the devastation ripping through me in my grief.

Now, I was quiet. Sitting in the van, staring out the window as Mike wound the van back through the cemetery, even the kids recognized the solemnity.

I took a deep breath, ready to return to the world of my family. While I continued to ask for proof, no longer did I sit paralyzed while I waited.

"Life is for the living," my dad had once told me. I tried to remember that.

I flipped the knob on the radio a little too far so the song blared out.

And if you go chasing rabbits, and you know you're going to fall...

Jefferson Airplane. *White Rabbit.* Really?

There wasn't much else I could do but laugh a little, shake my head and say, "Thank you, David."

I still didn't know the significance of a white bunny, but somehow it had become a sign of spirit.

***

Spring came and with it came a teacher's stress and pressure of standardized testing. On the third day, my homeroom class finished up a difficult math portion of the test. Because some took longer than others, I allowed them to read or draw when finished in order to ensure they remained quiet.

While I waited, I thought about David. Death, heaven, spirit communication, mediums, souls...all of these consumed my every free moment. When the bell signaled the end of testing for the day, my students shifted in their seats waiting for me to dismiss them.

"Be sure to take everything with you. Thank you for working so hard. Have a great rest of the day." I sent them on their way and turned to organize the testing supplies.

"I made this for you." One of my students stood at my desk holding out a sheet of paper.

A white bunny filled the lined notebook paper page. At the top right in big bubble letters he'd written DAVID.

Oh.

I stayed composed. No way would I tell a 7th grader (or anyone) why bunnies were significant to me.

"Matt, thank you. I have to ask, though. Why did you draw this?"

I couldn't even comprehend the coincidence of it all.

"I don't know," he told me. "I just got a sudden urge to draw a white bunny, name it David, and give it to you."

Really?

Cool.

Here's the drawing with the name blurred out. As I mentioned in the author's note, names have been changed…including David's.

Thank you, David.

It's a Real Thing

Early one morning, I lay in bed, reluctant to get up. The memories of David wrapped around me and kept me warm. Cozy. I felt such love. I couldn't understand feeling this love so strongly.

Thoughts rushed in. "I don't understand this love. It's so strong. It feels so real. Like it's real. It's a real thing. I mean tangible. It's like something I can hold and have. Something that I have to take and do something with. I don't understand this. It's a real thing."

And then I broke long enough to ask, "David, do you know what I'm saying? Do you understand?"

Later that day, I sat crying on the phone as another medium, Susan Sanderford, spoke with me. Without any background information, she'd told me David's name, mentioned his sense of humor, the importance he placed on his religion. And then came this:

Susan: You've been online a lot. You've been talking to other people. I get the image of him standing right behind you sometimes giving you the words to say.

Me: Okay.

Susan: I don't know if you've felt it like that, but from your heart sometimes just these wonderful things come that help people. Do you understand?

Me: Yeah.

Susan: He is standing right there oftentimes giving you those words.

Me: I have felt that.

Susan: Okay, and he says you've been wanting to hear him. Do you know what I mean? But it's been coming through your thoughts. His words have been coming through your thoughts. His feelings have been coming through your thoughts. And you've kinda been looking for it in other ways, but it's always been there, it's always been present coming through the thoughts. Does that make sense?

Me: Yes, it does.

Susan: Alright. And so that's kinda, in a way, you channel him, alright?

Me: Okay.

Susan: And you channel, the way he calls it, our love. Does that make sense?

Me: Yeah.

Susan: Because you had this really, really great love. He says he taught you how to love, and you taught him how to love. And that that, in itself, is one thing, not two separate things, and that one thing still lives on even though you aren't in each other's physical presence. And that you created it together, and it exists as a real thing. I've never had it come through like this before, but what he's saying, that love, that energy of that love exists as a real thing, and it surrounds you and it surrounds him, and it's almost like it's there for you to share. Had you not experienced the kind of love that you had, you wouldn't know how to give it out to other people, but now you're just giving it out in droves. Make sense?

Me (crying): Yeah, I'm trying.

Susan: I've never had it described in that way from a spirit that your love is an energy that will exist from time on end. Not just two people but it's something you created or birthed together, and he just wants you to know that's why you came together so you would know that kind of love.

Because I'm Here for You

I wandered through a crowd of people in what seemed to be the middle of town. However, I'd walked there from my grandma's country home, so I was a little confused.

I knew I was dreaming and wondered at the discrepancy in the distance. I walked down the dirt road and then suddenly I was moving in and out of buildings downtown.

Every corner, every face, every building, I searched for David.

Half a block down the street, I saw Jerry Seinfeld and thought, "Oh, there's Jerry Seinfeld." Who knows where that came from???? I looked across the street at one particular spot in the crowd and saw David standing there just as plain as can be. He smiled when he saw I'd noticed him. His beard was full and mostly gray.

I thought, "Hey, that's David. There's David!" I was so excited I woke up. Ugh! As I drifted back to sleep, I prayed, Please let me dream of David again.

A dream began again. I walked around a building still searching for David. I realized immediately I was dreaming again. "David, where are you?" I kept calling out to him.

A car coasted up next to me in the parking lot and the driver rolled down the window. It was David! I was so excited I woke up again. So frustrating.

I fell back to sleep and once again ended up in the parking lot. I began floating over the asphalt and across a field calling David's name. I 'flew' slowly over the area; I could see other people, but I couldn't find David.

I floated back to my grandmother's house and went inside. The crowd from town milled around out in the yard. I stepped out the front door, and I saw David coming up the tall staircase towards me. In the 'real' world, her house sat at the top of a long sloping driveway. My dream mind had added the stairs. I ran outside on the landing and watched as he walked all the way up to me to meet me. For some reason, he held a cane, but when he got to the top he threw it aside. As in the dream earlier, his hair was gray, but he no longer had a beard. I took in all of these details as I studied him and tried to determine whether he was really there in my dream or if I was just dreaming him.

He grabbed me and hugged me. I could feel him!

"Look, David came to visit. He can come to visit." I squealed to Christie, my boss, who had walked up beside us.

She peppered him with a million questions. "What's it like to be in spirit? How do you see other spirits? Why, if there are spirits all around can we not see all of them instead of just you?"

He laughed, the same low full laugh I will always remember, and answered her in thought and with such animated gestures. "You all can see me because I'm here for you. You can only see the spirits who are here just for you. Because you're with Julie, you can see me, too."

As he said my name, he reached for my hand. I grabbed him and was delighted I could feel him. Lacing my fingers through his, I stared into his eyes, just as blue than they'd ever been. Even more. He kissed me quickly, gave me an even quicker hug.

And then I woke up.

Seeing Sparkles

My sister and I sat together on my living room couch talking about this and that. Something above me caught my eye, and I glanced up. A tiny bright yellow sparkling light floated down towards me. Reflexively, I ducked. As I did, I noticed more sparklies falling down around me.

I tried not to let my sister notice that I wasn't paying attention. It wasn't long, though, before I felt compelled to reach up and try to touch a sparkle. I couldn't keep them a secret from her any longer.

"Do you see them?" I asked her.

She looked where I was reaching and then at my face. Gently, she shook her head. "See what?"

"I see sparkles."

I glanced at her and raised my eyebrows, questioning. Still, she shook her head. "I don't see them, Julie."

I peeked up again and saw two remaining sparkles fading out just before they reached my forehead.

Shrugging like it was no big deal, I jumped back in to the conversation. Later, I told Mike about it.

"I wonder if you have a brain tumor," he actually said. What?

"I don't think so."

He just stared at me.

Shaking my head at him, I told him, "Okay, if it keeps happening we can have me checked for a brain tumor."

I never saw sparkles again. However, I did a little research and learned that there is a common belief that the sparkles are angels or spirit. I had never heard that before. Just as many times before, something unusual happened to me and only after did I learn that it was a common spiritual manifestation.

Happy Valentine's Day

Early on a cold February morning, I rushed to finish getting ready for work. Mike had taken the kids since I had a late start day. Unfortunately, I took advantage of the late start and slept in way too late.

In only my bra and underwear, I stepped through the living room on my way to the kitchen to grab a cup of coffee.

Clank. Clunk. Crash.

Something fell off the back of the TV. Had the vibration of my steps knocked it off? I shrugged to myself and went to check.

As I bent over, flailing my arm around behind the entertainment center trying to find what had fallen, a feeling that's difficult to describe came over me. I felt David. I could so vividly imagine him laughing at me that it seemed he was there. I could just picture my underwear clad rear end sticking up in the air as I tried desperately to reach the fallen object and could feel him laughing at me so strongly, I actually said out loud, "Stop laughing at me, David."

My fingers touched the edge of something hard and with a little more wiggling to reach it, I pulled out a dark wood-framed picture that usually rested on the top right side of the TV.

"There. Now really, David. Stop laughing."

I shook my head and went on about my day.

‎★‎

Valentine's Day, just a week after the fallen photo:

I was crying. Again. I couldn't figure out how to deal with the actual literal pressure inside of me. I felt such overwhelming love and had no where to put it. How could David be dead? I just couldn't understand. And it hurt. It literally hurt inside. Something had been ripped out of me.

Walking across the stair landing on my way to my bedroom, I stopped for a moment. In just a few minutes, I planned on attending an online chat room run by a medium named Natalie. I had seen her read before, and she seemed like the real deal, at least as far as I could tell. I hadn't decided yet if there truly was a real deal, but I know I wanted it. Problem was, I didn't want to just 'believe' someone was the real deal. I wanted proof. I was so afraid that I wanted it so badly that I might see things that weren't factual. I didn't want to be made a fool.

As I stopped and stood there at the base of the stairs, I threw my hands up in the air. "Just come through tonight, David," I pleaded. "Come through and say Happy Valentine's Day, babe. I love you. Do that, and I'll believe everything."

Transcript from the Reading with Natalie (copied directly from the chat transcript. While I shortened the part with my grandma, I changed nothing from David's although I did add a few of my thoughts along the way):

Natalie: Who is watching that show Joan of Arcadia.

Me: I am. (but it was on…probably a good guess someone was watching it…trying to not be too gullible).

Natalie: There's a grandmother figure coming through. Is your grandmother passed?

Me: Yes. (Still not convinced…a grandmother? Come on.)

Natalie: You have a sister?

Me: Yes.

Natalie: Who has the baby passed?

Me: My sister. (Megan had a miscarriage)

Natalie: She says she has the baby with her.

Me: Okay. Good.

Natalie: She is bringing your grandfather through. He smoked a pipe?

Me: Yes. (and even still not convinced...everything fit, but...)

Natalie: I will leave this with you Hon (I learned this is not an uncommon way for a medium to end a reading, and I thought what? It's over already? I definitely felt that it was lacking, but then she went on)...someone liked pets animals Hon...Hold on someone else is here?

Julie: yes?

Natalie: soft heart for animals

Natalie: Julie?

Julie: someone else too? Yes

Natalie: gentleman passed

Julie: yes

Natalie: did he truly as he says it love animals

Julie: yes very much

Natalie: Ok he is here he said he would he he heard U now he says U are shaking

Natalie: I like his smile

Julie: yes I am

Natalie: ok?

Julie: and he has a beautiful smile

Natalie: He says he liked it too!

Julie: yes lol he would say that

Natalie: Feels like a love yes?

Julie: yes

Natalie: Love love love he says tell her I am ok Natalie he says...

Natalie: I like him he is polite sweet!

Julie: yes, very polite, very sweet

Natalie: Great guy sensitive and loving

Julie: oh yes

Natalie: He says happy valentines day baby I love ya

Natalie: Ok?

Julie: ok

Natalie: I made your wish!

Natalie: He says

Julie: oh yes exactly

Natalie: U wished what?

Natalie: he would come through

Julie: that he would come through and wish me happy valentine's day

Natalie: for heart day

Natalie: yes

Julie: wow

Natalie: he told me and then you said it

Julie: I've been telling him that all day

Natalie: he is there Hon right there with you

Julie: I feel him…at least I think I do. I question it away.

Natalie: Yes he is with you Picture flopped!

Natalie: shelf right hand side (I think) dark wood

Natalie: on the right!

Natalie: Dark like cherry wood

Julie: dark wood picture on the right?

Natalie: Julie?

Julie: yes dark like cherry wood (I had a picture frame close to the desk where I sat. I thought she was talking about it as I hadn't yet remembered the morning the photo fell from the TV)

Julie: tilted but not flopped

Julie: in front of me though up on the desk

Julie: crooked

Natalie: yes...will flop it already had one time before he said

Julie: oh yes (I was just realizing what picture she was talking about)

Natalie: He is there Hon...

Julie: that has happened

Natalie: YES!!

Natalie: see it is him..U needed proof he says

Julie: I always ask for proof lol

Julie: constantly

Natalie: and were you scantily dressed getting ready in the a.m. when this happened? Rushing around?

Julie: ummmmm yes

Natalie: lol...don't worry didn't show me JUST heard him say this

Julie: whew

Natalie: lol roflmao

Natalie: I didn't see he said tell her this ..

Julie: ok

Natalie: I said OH NO he said OH YESSSS

Natalie: lol

Natalie: he is cute

Julie: yes, I think so, too

Natalie: sends loads of love hon

Natalie: hugs too!

Natalie: Break. I will leave this with you Julie

Julie: ty so much Natalie

Natalie: Julie God Bless welcome

(hugs from other people in the chat room)

Natalie: Julie did he have dark hair hon...

Julie: yes dark hair

Natalie: Yes that's what I saw and beautiful white teeth

Julie: oh yes. That's him.

Happy Valentine's Day, Baby. I love ya. Just what I had asked for. Although, I'd asked for him to say 'Babe' and I love 'you' not 'Baby' and 'ya', so maybe it wasn't real. After all, it was Valentine's Day. Maybe Natalie just made all of that up.

Really, Julie? Shut up.

The fear of being wrong held me back and kept me from appreciating the magnitude of this message at the time. Eventually, I got over it. Thank God!

Automatic Writing

Natalie offered readings via email. She did something called automatic writing that I'd heard about but never experienced. Because I felt confident in the chat room Valentine's reading she gave me, I decided to give the email reading a try.

I'd only be out $30 if it stunk. Well, that and I knew it'd be a rough blow to whatever faith and confidence I'd gained. Still, I wanted to see.

At her website, I sent in my payment. Once she confirmed, I sent her two questions phrased just exactly as they are here. She had no other information about us other than what she might have remembered from the reading. She took the questions and channeled David. Within a week, she emailed his responses.

What did I mean to him?

I never in my life thought I would fall in love with her, but I did. She was little and sweet with the cutest nose dotted with freckles. She had a sweet smile and bright blue trusting eyes. Although I tried for the longest time not to love her, I couldn't stop. Julie.

She looked at me like the whole world revolved around me. I didn't want to disappoint her in any way, to let her down. I began to come up with ways to see her. I wanted to make her laugh. To show her the world. To teach her everything she needed to know, everything I knew. She trusted me and I let her down. I didn't say what needed to be said or do what needed to be done and for that I am so very sorry. We missed out on a lifetime together, but we have more. She doesn't know that but she hopes for it. I'm here again to teach her and to tell her it's true. Julie.

She doesn't need me, but she needs to know she's enough and I can teach her that. We are we, I say that because it is true. She is me. I am she. That's what it is. I go to her in dreams. So she'll know. Julie.

Where is he?

Here. Within you. I am a part of you. I am in you. I breathe for you and you for me. You are my air, my breath, my me. Whenever you go somewhere think of me and what I can do for you. Carry me with you as I do you. If I give you too much at once, you won't remember so little bits at a time. How there? How then? I wrote you a letter, I drove to see you. I sat outside not knowing what to do. I loved you. I didn't know how to say it, where to go with it. I didn't know. I wasn't perfect like what you saw me to be. I was just me. Just a man. I adored you. What was I supposed to do? I didn't know.

Now I know. Now I understand. It's bigger than we ever knew. A part of us, with us but more. I will help you understand too. Live big. Love big. I am still here for you. Use me, Julie. Use me to know and understand love. Share it. And then come home. Love. Love. It's love.

PART FIVE: What Did You Learn?

Peace

The point came when I quit questioning and just knew. Ten years of searching gave me the foundation and knowledge my soul needed to finally understand. How some people get it with just a sign or two, I don't know. Guess that's just me. I needed PROOF. Over and over and over again.

Peace entered my soul, and I allowed it to stay rather than kicking it out when fear and doubt tried to replace it. I understood the connection between the spirit within me and the Great Spirit outside of me. I am a part of that greatness, a part of God. The analogy of the water droplet in the sea reminds me of a person's connection with God. We all are a piece of that spirit making up the whole. Physical death doesn't change who we are. Only the education and experiences of our souls do that.

A sense of calm and contentment filled me. Imagine our endless possibilities when we recognize who we are. I craved that 'God-feeling' all the time. No longer did I feel conflicted between the idea of living with that feeling and having to live in the world now - having to deal with the earthly world struggles - ego, etc. Once I totally accepted who I am, I was able to let all of that go. I was free to just be me and for the first time in my life, I truly realized that if someone else had issue with me then that was on them. It really had nothing to do with me.

Whew. Talk about freeing.

World peace has become a mockery. It's said with raised eyebrows and skeptical tones like the person uttering the words doesn't really believe it can ever happen. Losing hope ensures it never will.

We search for peace outside of ourselves rather than knowing it resides within. We look to others for understanding and then wonder why those same others don't 'get it'. We try to mold and make and force everyone else to do and to be the way we think they should.

It's easier to look out than in. After all, our eyes point that way, don't they? We see what everyone else is doing wrong, and so it makes sense we'd want them to change instead of us.

Imagine a tree-lined mountain stream, water gently flowing, birds chirping, breeze blowing. Sounds peaceful. However, if I experience that scenario with fear or turmoil within me, I am not at peace no matter how gentle my surroundings are. Peace can never be found outside of ourselves, only reminders of peace can. Each individual has to experience it for themselves. How we feel within drives our actions, and all the people who look outside of themselves and wish for world peace need to only recognize that it starts with them.

Wouldn't it be wonderful to be reminders of peace for them?

We can each do that. Look inside; it's in the light that is you. Wrap your arms around it and allow it to consume you, encompassing you with such beauty and fulfillment that you'll completely understand an eternal perspective.

Lessons in All Forms

The saying, 'Time heals all wounds' really isn't accurate. Time doesn't heal anything. What you do with your time is what counts. Staying curled up in the fetal position for hours, days, years on end gets you no where.

It's interesting how the lessons I learn match the stages of my spiritual growth. From being too scared to believe anything to attributing spirit to only that which is outside of me, to understanding it all flows through me and is me, I've learned so much.

During the times I only recognized God as a separate but loving part of my life, I continued to reach for Him, searching, asking, moving, moving, moving. Almost frantic with the need to have Him, I jumped in to all kinds of activities trying to do something, make a difference, feel Him.

I 'loved' so much. I could feel my love for David and his for me. Right away, I understood that this was the unconditional love all the spiritual people were talkin' about. But when you feel something so deeply, you also think you have to do something with it - something more than just *love*.

It wasn't just a feeling, an emotion. No, this love was tangible with a life of its own. I knew it didn't only belong to me, so it seemed selfish to hoard it. Surely I had to actively pursue giving it away.

When I realized God is in me all the time, I could finally slow down and begin to learn to just be. While my life can remind (remember the mountain stream?) others of peace and love, I can not take on the whole world and make everyone else feel the same way. God is in them all the time, too. I'm no different than anyone.

I share my lessons in the stages I received and interpreted them wanting to make clear that not everything happened in perfect order. Two steps forward, one step back. Three steps forward, 12 steps back - that's how I roll. But for the most part, the forward journey continues.

Blondin/Trust

Life moves along. Houses need cleaned, salaries must be earned, husbands want attention, children need food and taxi service and hugs and kisses. Recognizing the hope and peace and joy within in us is only the beginning. Knowing Him isn't enough. I prayed every day, "God, I know you're real. How do I use this knowledge and put it into action. What do I do?"

Several years had passed. Too many signs, coincidences, readings, visions, had happened for me to deny. I knew God was behind it all, but I didn't yet understand what that meant for me. I felt compelled to act on the knowledge but didn't know where to begin.

David told a story once about a tightrope walker from the late 1800s named the Great Blondin. Blondin walked across the Niagara Falls multiple times, always theatrical, always with crowds cheering him on. One day after he finished his walk across, the audience went wild, but Blondin silenced them. As soon as they quieted, he said, "I am the Great Blondin. Do you believe?" Everyone shouted in unison, "We believe. Yes, we believe!" He says, "I am the greatest tightrope walker in the world. Do you believe that?" The crowd shouted, "Of course, we believe, we believe!" He said, "Do you believe that I can get a wheel barrow and put it in front of me and put someone in that wheel barrow and walk back across the Niagara Falls?"

Everyone had seen his feat already and they said, "Of course, we believe. We believe."

Blondin says, "Okay, then who will be my volunteer?"

Wow. That's it. No one said anything. It was total silence. Nobody said anything. No one volunteered.

Finally, one man in the back raised his hand. This lone man said, "I believe you can do that, and I'll do that. I trust in you." The man got in the wheel barrow and Blondin pushed him all the way across the Niagara Falls and back.

As I tried to figure out what to do with my belief in God, I considered this story. It pretty much summed up my relationship with God. It's one thing to say I believe. Yes, I believe in God. It's an entirely different matter to trust the one we say we believe in. Believing is not just saying I accept the facts. Believing is like that man who said I am going to put my trust in the one I say I believe in. Do we trust the One we say we believe in?

Trusting opens us up to vulnerability. That's scary! But if we allow our relationship with God to reach a whole new level, then we no longer merely believe. We know He's real. And if He's real, then all His promises are real, too.

Yes, Lord!

Trust. I trust God.

I stood by my bed and raised my hands up in the air. "Lord," I offered myself. "I'm ready. Whatever you want, Lord. I say yes. Yes, Lord." At that moment the song, "Trading My Sorrows" by Darrell Evans came to mind – "Yes, Lord, Yes, Lord, Yes, Yes, Lord." I sang the few lines I knew and danced around the room while I promised God I'd do whatever He wanted.

And then I added a couple of disclaimers (you know you do it, too), "And Lord, if possible, maybe whatever you ask of me could have to do with speaking to women…but most of all, whatever it is, please make it clear enough that I recognize it's from you."

Other than in teaching, I'd never used my public speaking degree. I felt ready to move into action. Maybe God was working in my life all along, even back in college when I chose my major. Maybe he was preparing me so that when He called, I would be ready. That's a thought worth thinking about.

Next morning, I rolled over, grabbed my phone, and checked my email. My pastor's wife had written me. She had been invited to speak at a women's retreat. Having never done this before and not really liking to speak to people, she immediately began praying about it.

In her email she wrote:

I thought maybe I could get a girlfriend or two (one who I know is comfortable talking in front of people) to go with me and share the speaking/teaching. "Julie" came to my mind!... Soooooo...... I'm asking you to pray about going with me.

Pray about it? I thought. I didn't need to pray about whether or not I should do it. I had already prayed about it. I prayed about it BEFORE she asked me. I'd already said, Yes, Lord. And, He made it clear to me.

Out of My Comfort Zone

I continued clinging tightly to my Bible and carrying it everywhere with me, and I began feeling compelled to do things. I frequently recalled David, sitting in his car with his head in his hands, whispering, "You can't help but be motivated to do something." I finally understood what he meant.

When my local women's group asked me if I would consider being their president, I jumped in and said yes. I also decided to be Team Captain for a Relay for Life team. Both of these new leadership roles definitely pushed me way out of my comfort zone. I was a follower, never a leader. I didn't know enough to be a leader.

With both roles, I found myself very busy, learning new things, sometimes overwhelmed, but still enjoying the feeling of contributing. Something (God) worked inside of me and kept me moving, understanding that these kinds of things were how I was being called to serve. Being useful in His name would be where purpose could be found.

Around this same time, I began a graduate degree which called for another eight to ten hours per week of my time. And, I became a Hospice volunteer.

God really led the way and reminded me of His infinite patience when it came to my experience with Hospice. I kept trying not to listen to Him, though. I began thinking about David's death, about cancer and the whole process of dying. I wondered if I might be able to help someone facing his own death. I hadn't been able to help David in those two or three months he was dying, a fact I struggled to come to grips with. If I could help someone else, though, in honor and memory of David, that might ease my grief.

The idea of Hospice scared me. Talk about out of my comfort zone. I had never done anything like helping anyone, much less a stranger, through the dying process. Although the idea floated around in my head, I refused to grab hold of it and pursue it. Oh, I did at one point say, "Okay, God. I'll try to call Hospice and see what I need to do to volunteer." But then I only half-heartedly searched the phone book for the number. When I didn't find it in the first couple of places I looked, I shrugged to myself and just thought, "Oh well." I was too scared to dig any further.

I tried to put it out of my head. I didn't really want to volunteer for Hospice anyway. Did I?

A few weeks later, I still couldn't get the thought of volunteering for Hospice out of my mind. Again, I halfway attempted to find their number and again gave up when I didn't find it quickly.

I moved on to other things and tried not to think about it anymore.

Mike and I sat in our living room watching Jeopardy a few weeks later. I finally gave in…a little. "Mike," I said. "I can't stop thinking about Hospice. I'm going to have to find their number and call."

Mike agreed. "When you can't get a thought out of your head like that, someone is trying to get you to listen."

I wasn't totally sure about that, but I knew I needed to look forward into what was next in my faith journey. "After dinner tonight, I'll search harder for the number," I told him.

We planned to go to our church that evening for dinner before the kids had choir and Bible study. I decided I'd find the number when we returned home.

We could smell fried chicken as soon as we stepped in the church door. Quickly, we fell in line, anxious to get our plates. Just to the right of the food table, a bulletin board hung on the wall. I'd passed that bulletin board countless times. This time, as we stepped past, a paper hanging in the middle caught my eye. It was the only paper on the entire board. I stepped closer and looked at it. "Volunteers for Hospice Needed", the headline read. Underneath was a description of the duties involved and below that, sectioned off in neat little tear-off pieces, was the phone number to call. I could not believe what I saw. The number for Hospice? Really? With that kind of timing? Knowing at that moment just what God was trying to tell me, I ripped one of those little strips off the flyer and tucked it away in my pocket. Silently, I prayed, "Thank you, Lord. I will call. I promise."

Within the week, I kept my promise and called. I'm so glad I did. Something else happened with my Hospice experience that both amazed and humbled me. Before I was able to work with a patient, I had to go through extensive training. Each Tuesday and Thursday for six weeks, I left my teaching job at the end of the day and went straight to the Home Health Care office where I attended Hospice Volunteer Training. Training was an emotional time for me, and I often wondered if my trainer noticed that I frequently had to wipe away my tears. It wasn't only that I was sad. I was so grateful to feel like I was answering God's call, to feel like I was doing something. Purpose is found in what we do in His name. I finally began to realize that.

And God let me know specifically that He continued to be with me.

When it came time for me to finally meet my first patient, my trainer and I met outside of the nursing home where I would be visiting. We sat out on a little bench as we went through confidential paperwork. This particular patient had cancer and Alzheimer's. She was 99 years old. Her family, who lived only about 20 miles away, just wanted someone to visit her in the off times they couldn't be there. That would be my job.

Then, the trainer pulled out the last sheet of paper. "Let's see, Julie," she said to me. "This patient will be 100 on..." her eyes scanned the page, and then she continued, "July 17. July 17 is her birthday."

July 17. Two days after my birthday. The anniversary of David's death. Another coincidence that was not lost on me. Well, let me take that back. I noticed it. It mattered. I was amazed by it. And while I didn't lose it, I misplaced it for a while. I didn't trust enough to keep it with me. Only now, can I look back and understand the enormity of that coincidence. These types of universal alignments began to guide me as I came to trust them as signs that I was on the right track in whatever path I took. I thanked God and kept moving forward the best I could.

Balance

Feeling like I was answering God's call to do something in His name felt great. However, I began to struggle with the time commitment. I came home exhausted. Housework, checking over children's homework, time for myself to read or relax all became things of the past. It wasn't long before I came to resent having to go; I wanted to stay home and take care of myself and my family. I felt guilty if I sat still too long, spent too long reading a book, let a day go by only doing things for me. I should be out doing.

Due to the pressure, I dropped out of all my extras. I finished my classes; my Hospice stint ended when my supervisor moved away; my term as women's group president expired. And I did nothing to replace those things. For a while, when not working or caring for my family, I just sat mindlessly in my recliner playing computer games, not wanting to invest myself in much of anything emotionally. I still completed all the necessary tasks, but I couldn't bring myself to step out and get involved again.

I continued praying. Opening my Bible, I read scriptures about all of the times Jesus went to the mountain to pray. Those scriptures opened me to the understanding that we all need that time to refresh and renew our relationship with God. It is not only okay but necessary to stop and pray. And I reminded myself that praying wasn't just talking at God but remembering to be still and listen.

Without nurturing ourselves, it's impossible to be involved and not get overwhelmed. I didn't know how to take care of my home and family and still have the energy to help anywhere else. Resentment and fatigue are not a part of God's plan. Slowly, I came to the realization that I had to be first - oh, not first before God - just first - with God. I had to nurture my relationship with Him so that I was healthy on the inside. In addition, I had to tend to myself so that I was healthy on the outside. Only then, could I truly take care of my family. And if that was as far as I could reach – myself and my family – then that was okay, too. Little bits at a time, I worked on myself and my relationship with God. Then, I began figuring out how to share that relationship with my family. Only then was I ready to broaden my scope and again step outside of my most familiar surroundings to find a place where I could help others in His name.

Caught Up in Purpose

If I get caught up in 'I have to do this because it's my purpose' then soon I become overwhelmed. Instead, I need to just be. When I am true to my light within, my light will lead me in the path and time frame

I need to go for what is best for my soul. As soon as I start trying to think it through, ego becomes involved. The minute I think, 'I have to do this today', I begin to panic and stress. I can't sit idly and expect spirit to take over. I have to make a conscious effort to know and find my peace within. And then follow. When I do that, all will be well.

David Appears

Birds chirped outside the window. They sounded so happy. Ugh. I groaned in the pitch dark. The sun hadn't even begun to lighten the morning sky and yet I was awake early once again. I'd been waking up earlier and earlier for weeks. I longed for the days of sleeping past 5:00 a.m. It was official; I'm old.

My stomach tightened, and my chest swelled. Immediately, I thought of David. I'd come to attribute this feeling to him. Right before feeling his presence, I'd feel this feeling. "Hi, David," I thought the words instead of saying them out loud and then tried to blank my mind so that I might hear something back. Over time, I learned to do this. In the beginning, I asked for the thoughts I'd 'hear' to be something I didn't know, that I could validate later. That was part of asking for proof.

That happened enough, and I'd begun to believe. Because I was a visual learner, though, there was still always a tiny bit of doubt at the back of my mind. It could be possible I was just making it all up. Maybe.

"Open your eyes."

The words penetrated my mind, interrupted my thoughts.

"Open your eyes."

Slowly, I responded, peeking through slits unsure if I made the words up or if I really heard them from outside of me. Or inside of me. It's confusing to describe.

Beside my bed and about four feet off the ground, a light penetrated the darkness. It was blue and had no shape to it at first. I shook my head, squeezed my eyes shut, opened them again. The light remained.

"It's me." I heard the whisper, still in my head.

"David?"

The light began to take shape. It stretched and spread out and while the edges never became sharp, the form was definitely that of a person. I couldn't see any details. Just light.

But I felt him. "David!"

I wanted to jump up, to grab him. I'd only seen him in dreams and even though I'd long had enough proof many of those dreams were actual visits, there was always that minute possibility that I was just making him up. I wanted him so badly. It made sense that I could just be fooling myself. Didn't it?

"Sh. Be really still. Remember how you wake yourself up in a dream when you focus on the physical? Don't do that now."

"Wake myself up? Am I dreaming?"

"No, but if you jump to touch me, if you focus on physical, you'll blanket your spiritual connection. You know the phrase 'be in the moment?' Think about that, but instead of 'moment' think 'feel'. Be in the *feel*. Feel me and you'll see me with spiritual eyes. I'm afraid you'll stop seeing me otherwise." He laughed then. "And I've worked very hard to get you to see me. But I'm still learning, too."

I lay back but kept staring as his light became sharper and clearer. It was all I could do to not reach out and try to grab him. How I longed to touch him.

"How do you do that? How are you doing that?"

His face was clear enough I could see his smile now. "I don't know. Concentration, I think. That combined with you being ready. Finally." He teased me. He was teasing me. David crossed dimensions and immediately teased me.

Typical.

Wonderful.

"Why did you take so long to get here? I was ready a long time ago."

He shook his head. "You thought you were ready, but too many things tied you down here. Doubt, fear. The normal stuff."

"This is crazy."

"You think so?" He grinned again.

"Probably." I didn't know what to think about my sanity, but I knew for a fact I could see him. I'd been hearing him so long, asking for proof for so long. And now here he was.

I wanted tangible, and while I couldn't hold him, well…actually seeing him was tangible enough for me.

"I love you so much," I whispered.

He nodded. "I feel it."

"So what took you so long?" I had to tease him, too.

"I've been yelling at you for years. You couldn't hear me."

I thought about that for a minute. "I heard something."

He stood there grinning at me, just watching me.

"Huh," I chuckled. "I thought God was talking to me. I thought you were God."

He raised his eyebrows at me. "Maybe I am."

"Psshh." If I could have swatted him, I would have.

But I thought about it. "Where is God? How does that work?"

"God is here. And there." He tilted his head to the left. "And there." To the right. "God is everywhere, everything, everyone."

"I love you, David." I had to tell him again. It's the only time I'd ever been able to say it to his face. "I love you so much. I get it. I get it now. I'm supposed to use this love here. To make the earth better. To make it 'His kingdom.' Right? That's what that means. That's what Jesus was talking about."

His face.

Oh, his face.

For the first time in close to 25 years somebody was looking at me like every word I said was important. His expression, slight grin, bright eyes watching me closely. I'd forgotten what it was like to feel so accepted. So important.

Whether what I said was right or not, I knew David would never make fun of my ideas, never criticize my thoughts. He agreed with me now, though.

"That's right. It's love, and it is what Jesus was talking about. It's what He meant when He said the kingdom of God is here. It's here, Julie. I'm here. We're here. It's all happening right now.

"It's in you and always has been. It's who you are, your very nature. You, like so many others, made the mistake in thinking it was in someone else. But it's been in you all along.

"I came to teach you that. I didn't really understand either. Not completely. I was always just a little bit ahead of you in where I was, leading you, trying to show you the way, but there was so much more for me to learn and to know. Still is. I'm learning now and taking you with me as quickly as I can. Dragging you when I have to."

I grinned, embarrassed at the need to drag me but knowing it was true.

"It's pretty cool, isn't it?" I asked him. "Tell me. Tell me what it's like. I mean, after you died. After the dying…were you surprised you were still alive?"

"Pleasantly. I found you right away."

"I was a mess."

He shook his head. "No, not a mess. Dead inside. Somewhere along the way you let life cover up your joy. The energy of knowing how much you're loved was missing. You'd lost it, let it be covered up, even though so many people love you.

"I'm helping others who are the same. Counseling them. Helping them see the bigger picture of love. I can relate to them because they're us. When you know the fullness of love, you can fully live again. I want to teach you that."

"Thank you. I want to know. I want to know everything. But sometimes I…" I trailed off. I wanted to seem only spiritual, like all that mattered to me was learning about my own energy and spirit and what to do with it, but I remembered David. The feel of his hand on mine. His expression when I touched him. The comfort and safety I felt in his arms. I still wanted that, too. It wasn't fair we lost that.

"It's fair, Julie. Everything is fair. It's just the way it is. How do we react to it? What do we do with it? No matter the circumstance, we take it and go with it."

"How did you do that? I didn't say that out loud. I didn't even think it to you!" I knew I didn't have to talk for him to hear me, but I did kind of think I at least had to want him to hear what I was thinking.

Laughing again at me, he said, "I've always known what you're thinking. Almost always. And now, I am your thoughts. You're mine. We're the same energy. All of us are. You and I are just tuned in a little more. We can do that, you know? It's pretty neat."

I shook my head at him and laughed, too. "Super. I have no secrets."

"There's no need."

He was fading a little. "Do you have to go? I don't want you to go. In a minute, okay? But not now."

"Shh." He comforted me. "I'm in no hurry. There's no time here."

I sighed in relief.

"So what do we do?" I still wasn't exactly sure how I was supposed to use what I know in my world. My earthly world. What was the point really?

"You're going to know that you are love."

"I don't know, David, but I'll try. I'd do anything for you."

"Then live," he told me. "I'll tell you what it's like. What it's all about. You take that information out there and live."

I pulled my blankets up tight around my chin and closed my eyes. I didn't know if I could do it without him. But I wasn't really without him, was I? Wasn't that the point? And even if I was, this love, this energy, this power…it was in me anyway. As an individual, I had as much God in me as anyone. It wasn't dependent on anyone.

I had to think about it. I reopened my eyes and looked once more at the face I'd loved since I was 16 years old.

"Think about it," David said. He'd heard my thoughts again. Guess that was going to be an every moment thing.

"I want to know everything. How will you teach me? Will I always see you?"

"Sometimes. Maybe. Mostly you'll hear me, feel me, dream me. Like you've been doing for a while. You just needed a boost this time."

"Okay."

"I love you, Julie."

At that moment, I realized I no longer needed the words. I'd doubted what I meant to him for so long because of our earthly situation and because I'd never heard him say the words. But I felt him now, felt his love. It intermingled with my love for him, swelled together and wrapped itself around me. It filled my chest, my entire insides until I was swollen with love. It made sense there would be so much that it would burst out of me into the world. That's what it was about. If I feel it that much, I can't help but put it out there. It couldn't be contained inside of me.

I smiled at him and saw that the light that he was had begun to dim.

"By the way," I heard him, but the thought seemed far away. "I miss that, too."

I felt his smile, his energy, as the last bit of light faded away and I was left to lay there and contemplate the possible journey ahead of me.

It's in You

I'm dreaming in visual darkness but full of David's presence. I hear him and listen intently. It's important. It's always important.

"You think it feels right and that is because it is. I knew this was in you...always. It's you and it's God together. That's how it works, and those who get things done recognize this. Sometimes people take the credit, but those who do have more burnout and fade out than those who don't.

"Let God lead, and you will find all you have ever looked for and hoped for. Including me because I am a part of that. Do I mean I wouldn't love you if you didn't listen? No. Not at all. I will always love you...but this is what we are made for...from the inside, knowing God, that we are a part of Him, letting that part shine through us, through our physical bodies. Together. Whole. This is us, Julie. It's who we are. Who everyone is. Being God...with God. A part of God. Think about it."

Come Here

Laying in bed, eyes closed, I think of David. Whoosh, I feel him. Just like that. He always made an entrance.

I open my eyes and see him standing at the foot of my bed; he's wearing jeans and a bright yellow shirt. I realize there must be significance in the color he's wearing. I've come to determine he uses color to send me messages even though he's never said as much. They're such a strong part of my visions, I feel it's true.

I notice he's wearing blue jeans. Nice.

"I like you in khakis, too," I tell him.

He grins. "I know."

Then, he says to me, "Come with me, Julie."

"What? Where?" I ask him.

"Come see me."

"But you're here," I tell him. "We're here together, right? This...it's real."

"Yes, it's real," he nods at me. "But there's more. I can come all the way there, or we can 'meet' in the middle like this. But you can also come here. I want you to come here to me. I want to take you farther. I want to show you more."

"David, I don't understand."

"I can't touch you here in the in between. Not really. We can only think about it, and that's fine, but if I come all the way there or you all the way here then we can touch each other."

"Can you kiss me?" What? Judge me, I'm human. Just tellin' it like it is here.

He grinned. "I can, but I won't. It's not about that. You know it. Otherwise, I would."

"I know it." Sigh.

"It's never been about that." He was still grinning at me.

"I thought it was," I told him.

He nodded. "Me too. We don't always know so much when we're housed in those bodies. We can feel it. A little of it. Some. We know it's there and that we're supposed to do something with it; we just don't quite know what."

So that meant no kissing. Yes, I got more out of it than that. I have grown up a little. Promise.

Still.

"But if I can come there I can really feel? I could really feel your hand? Or your face?"

"Yes."

All of sudden, I realized that his request was similar to a request he made so many years ago. "Come see me, Julie," he said to me then. He wanted me to drive to him. To make that move…to go to him. I didn't do it. Fear of not belonging in his world is perhaps what held me back. I'm not sure. I wish now, though, that I had gone. That he'd known how much he meant to me.

Am I still going to let the fear of not belonging in his world hold me back?

"This is like before. Only I didn't go."

He nodded again. "I wish you would have."

"So do I."

"What if I don't come now?" I asked him.

"What if you don't?" He was very matter of fact. No anger, no anything.

"Will you still love me?"

"I will always love you."

I stood for a minute, and he spoke again, "But I'd like you to come. You're ready for more. I want to show you more."

I felt that. I always felt like David wanted to share with me. Like he wanted to teach me and show me all the things he knew. It felt the same way now.

"I'll try, David. I'm afraid I can't get there, though."

"Quiet your mind. Use music if you need…your meditation CDs. You can get here," he told me.

I lay my palm on his cheek and remember feeling the rough stubble of his beard. "I'll come," I said.

He smiled.

Later, I searched for meanings of colors in dreams. Yellow indicates focus and awareness and reminds us of our role as humans within the context of the whole. It's the color of intelligent design. Yellow paves the way to a path of higher understanding and mystical awareness. It centralizes our energetic focus so that we may intensify our presence.

Made Up of Light

Early in the morning a week later, I woke up to David.

"Come here. Come here." The insistence in his voice kept me from thinking anything else.

"It's too late," I said. "I'm already awake. It's too late to dream you."

I knew he meant meditation, though. I reached for my iPad and one of my favorite meditation tracks. I settled in with my headphones and as the music began to play, I tried to direct my thoughts. It was such a hard thing to not try to guide the meditation. I knew it had to do with my need for control. I have to work on that every single time.

I heard David again. "Quit thinking and let it be."

"Okay, okay."

Within the blackness of my closed eyes, I saw him appear in brilliant bold light. Every color stood out vividly. His eyes, always beautiful blue, piercing and brighter than I'd ever seen.

He was showing me he was made up of light. While he'd appeared as light in my bedroom the first time I'd seen him, I hadn't realized he actually was light.

"I get it," I told him. "You are a body made of light. You're real and made of light."

As I thought that to him, a lesser dense light spread out from his body. It reminded me of the halos of light I see around car headlights at night. It began to spread out in all directions and in all colors going this way and that. Then, he shattered. His body pixelated and each fleck of light scattered in a million different directions. I watched carefully. Observing.

Pixel by pixel each piece came back together until his body was once again complete. He stood next to me.

"What did you learn?" David asked.

"You are made up of light. And so am I, but mine is inside my physical body. The solidity of spirit is a concentrated light, where the focus is intensified to make the colors brighter. For you to appear. For your body to be.

"I can focus on my body of light within me, too. Through concentration, meditation, understanding of my energy, then I can allow my light body to lead me as it is what's true and real. It is what's eternal."

Everything went black and the music playing reached my ears again. I listened for a few more moments and another picture began to form in my mind.

A lake loomed in front of me. David and I sat on the edge of a dock, feet dangling over, toes dipped into the dark water. I felt a presence behind us and lifted my head to see who it was.

Jesus stood and spread his arms and wrapped them around our shoulders, both of us cocooned within his embrace.

"Is this okay, Jesus?" I had been worrying about religion. And spirituality. It didn't seem right that they couldn't go hand in hand, but all the rules I'd always learned made it seem like they didn't. "Is this okay? Is it okay that I connect to you, to God, with David...through David?"

His gentle words filled me even more. "As long as it is love, it is good. Real. Right. That's who I am."

My heart filled with the same fullness and feeling of love David had shown me so many times. His arms pulled in tighter and held us close letting us know that we are a part of Him. Growing together with Him and for Him and to Him.

I opened my eyes and no longer saw them, but the feeling stayed with me for a long time. Even now.

Another Visit

The bathtub became a perfect place for me to quiet my mind. David always seemed to know as soon as my brain was still. He would jump right in and tell or show me something new.

I lay back and closed my eyes. Sure, I had to get past the fear of connecting with David while I was in the bathtub. Oh no! And then I reminded myself (a million times) that if I really thought it was all about being naked in the bathtub then I wasn't really learning any lessons at all. Ha.

As I connect with spirit, there are two types of thoughts I deal with with my eyes closed. One I call external thoughts. Yes, they're still in my head, but they seem to come from my brain, from thinking. They are worldly and get in the way. Then, there are my internal thoughts, the ones I don't really have to think about. They just appear; besides just thinking them, I feel them. They are a part of me. Inside of me. Those are the thoughts that come from spirit.

I see the darkness, and I think too hard trying to get there. David again guides me, soothes me, helps me relax.

I hear his whisper back behind my external thoughts. "Sh. Quiet. Listen. Listen to me. To what I'm saying."

I shift my focus to his whispers and allow the external to fall away.

I'm standing in a dark room. The color red appears. It's all around. It's not anything he's wearing, though. I don't see David at all. Only red in the darkness. Later, I learn that red stands for passion, aggression, going for it. Giving it all.

I'm scared I can't do this, can't make it to the other side in meditation. Or what if I get there and can't figure out how to be a part of it?

"Shh." Once again, I'm comforted by his voice.

A pinpoint of light shines through the wall of darkness. I watch as it gets a little bigger, the size of a baseball.

I feel David there beside me. He loves me no matter what. He wants to show me more, to teach me more. I don't have to be scared anymore.

He reaches out and I see only his hand as it slips into the baseball size brightness, grips the sides, and pulls it open.

"What do you see?" he asks me.

"I can't see you." You can tell what I was concerned about.

"It doesn't matter yet."

Green. I could see green pastures. In the not too far distance I see our tree. The large oak tree we once picnicked under after our trek across the field of pasture grass the time he laughed at me for wearing my sandals.

"You put my tree there for me!"

"Where do you want to go?" he asks.

"To the tree."

We're there just like that.

I hear a dog bark and from around the tree, a black lab runs to greet me.

"Annie!" Our Little Ann died last November. She was here. "You have Annie?"

"Only for now. She's mine for now, but she'll go with Mike when he gets here. She loves Mike. And no hurry on that. She's good. She's happy."

I was amazed.

"Show me more."

His shirt appears to me, earthy browns, oranges. It's plaid. That's all I can tell. "What's that mean?" I don't want to wait until I can research it to know.

"Balance. Freedom."

Oh. I'll have to think on that.

"That's all," David tells me. He reaches for my hand, and I feel him. I can feel his touch. Surprised, I quickly look up at him. He smiles, and I open my eyes.

Color research after a dream with specific colors is always a must. I was especially curious about the orange and brown plaid especially since David told me balance and freedom. I was surprised and pleased to find both of those words in the descriptions of the colors:

Orange – sign of equalization, balance, and temperance. Orange is the fulcrum and our perception the teeter-totter. Consider what is in balance or in need of balance.

Brown - signifies freedom, success, money and happy and long-lasting union. Brown also represents the ground and earth. You need to get back to your roots.

About Dad

I close my eyes when I meditate, quiet my mind, and basically just watch to see what happens. I don't believe it mandatory for eyes to be closed, but I'm new enough to it all that it helps me to focus. Otherwise, distractions get in the way.

As more spiritual events occurred, I studied harder learning all I could about energy, connection with spirit, meditation. I set my intention to open my third eye and to be open to anything that came through. I specifically set the intent that it didn't have to be David. I don't want to try to control what I *think* I should see. I merely want to observe.

I practiced frequently. In the beginning, I had a hard time keeping my eyes closed, and I would see my living room through the slits in my eyes. I tried to let go and not think about anything, but external thoughts invaded my spiritual brain space. Would I see anything? What if I did? What would it be? What if I didn't? Hey, did I remember to put the laundry in the dryer?

One morning, I sat thinking about Natalie, the medium who'd given me the chatroom reading on Valentine's Day and the channeled automatic writing so many years before; I felt her presence which made no sense to me as I didn't know her to have passed. Her spirit felt calm and loving.

"You helped me," I told her.

She just smiled, and I felt comforted and peaceful. I was thankful I had a chance to tell her.

Then I felt David. He came in stages. First, I felt his smile and his eyes. I saw the vivid blue in his eyes. Piercing. He reminded me of love and home. He wore faded blue jeans and a white button down shirt. His brown hair fell loosely over the tops of his ears and his forehead. His lower face was scruffy as if he hadn't shaved for a couple of days.

"You look gorgeous." I told him. He smiled wider.

"Thank you."

I grinned back at him and then stepped close to him. He wrapped his arms around me and hugged me.

"You're gorgeous." I repeated. I couldn't seem to feel him enough or see him enough. I couldn't get enough of him. But it wasn't him; not really. It was that love. I couldn't get close enough to that unconditional love.

I felt him grin.

"Why did I see Natalie?" I was curious.

"You are seeing those who have passed who have and will help you in your journey. You will keep seeing them."

I lay my head on his chest for just a moment and we stood there briefly, and then he pulled away. "Come with me." A bench sat off to the side within a small circle of flat rocks laid out on the ground. We sat down, and I pressed up against him, He took my hand.

"Look over there." He nodded his head forward, directing my attention in front of us. The ocean stretched out forever, waves gently lapping up onto the beach. In between our bench and the water, a huge rock sat. A dark haired woman wearing a long flowing white dress sat about halfway up the side of it.

"Do you recognize her?" David's voice was low.

I was in awe. "It's my mother."

David smiled. "Isn't she beautiful? So beautiful."

214

And she was. Her dark hair swept back behind her in the wind. Her dress did the same. She looked peaceful and content.

I was filled with such joy. Joy in seeing my mother, joy in feeling David's emotion. "She's waiting for your dad. There's no hurry. She's content and will wait as long as it takes. She always has. There's no time. No rush. They'll be together again."

"What about my mom?" I asked, meaning my stepmother, of course.

David answered carefully. "Oh, he loves her, too. It's a strong love full of respect and appreciation. It's real, but it's not the same. Your dad needed her strength when your mother left. They've been good for each other."

I sat, still holding his hand, and thought about that. I understood what he was saying. Different love is still love. You can love someone just as much as another only not in the same way.

I thought about Mike and how much I love him.

Yes, I understood exactly.

Also, I did a little research later. Natalie did pass away a few years before from cancer. I hadn't known that.

Base Spirit and Angels

David liked to appear early in the morning. Knowing I didn't have to speak out loud meant I didn't need to worry about waking Mike.

David would tell me or show me something and then ask, "What did you learn?"

"I learned about the 'base' spirit and how it all comes together. I learned that light bodies are still bodies. I learned the intensity of how you love me and all that encompasses. How you'll guide me so that I'll understand this kind of love is with everyone and for everyone.

"I learned that people in spirit are called angels and can help those on earth, but there are also celestial beings who have never been on earth in a body.

"I know that I am experiencing the magnitude of the light that is you. An immense, expansive light shining out everywhere. It reminds me of the light Zach described surrounding you when he first saw you after you died. That same light is housed in each of us. Our physical bodies hold it in, and our ego based fears, dreams, and desires can block it from ourselves and from the rest of the world. As we shed those things, our light shines brightly. We feel more deeply and spread God's love and joy to all of those we touch.

"I learned that I can trust. You, my meditations. I've had so much proof that I no longer need to ask for it. It's all been proven and now, even when I can't see, faith carries me through. When I see, there's no need for faith because that's what faith is, knowing something is true even when we can't see.

"You want to feel what I feel and see what I see, and you want me to do the same. I can trust that. I can live fully and boldly with that."

He smiled and nodded. "What will you do today?"

I thought about it a minute. "I don't know. I want to stay here with you. I want to feel like this all the time."

"You can. Take it. Go and love in all you do. Take me with you. Our lights together shine brighter than either one of us alone. Shine our lights together and see what good you can add to the world.

"Each person is his own light. Add that light with others and the brightness can overcome all darkness."

"Are you sure you can stay with me? Don't you need to go? Shouldn't you be in Heaven?"

He grinned, "I am in Heaven. I'm with you."

I rolled my eyes. "Oh, pssh." There was the old David. He might be some sort of bigger, wiser than ever spiritual guide now, but he was still David.

Now, he laughed at me. "Heaven is where the love is, Juliebean. It's here with me. It's in a cool summer breeze. It's with your family, your closest friends. It's in Charlie curled up in your lap."

Charlie's my son's cat. I do love when she's curled in my lap.

Heaven is love. Here or there.

Part of the Holy Spirit

"Be careful not to get caught up in the rules of religion or else you run the risk of missing the love.

Our spirit is part of the whole - a part of the Holy Spirit. We are just one little aspect of it - still magnificent in our own right - a little piece of the whole. We're even greater when we join our lights with others; then, we're closer to the whole which is God.

Darkness is easier because it's of earth, and we are here on earth. The light is heavenly, and that part of ourselves is more difficult to access because the dark/physical/earth covers it up. When we shed the physical, we are pure light and are then Heaven.

There is a dark force. Its very nature is the earthly/physical trying to cover the light. Some choose the dark because of its ease. Others acknowledge the light but don't think they can reach it; ego causes them to believe they don't deserve it. And still others strive to allow the light to cover up the darkness - strive to share the light with others. Think about a pitch dark room. One tiny light can be seen. A difference can be made."

Suicide?

"Killing yourself wouldn't bring you any closer to me. It's all about our spiritual closeness, and that can be learned whether we're physical or not. If the earthly body dies, we would still have to learn to be closer spiritually; it's all the same.

How do we do this? For us, it's consistent meditation, taking care of the physical self to be healthier, prayer, trusting God, loving each day, accepting His love. For two or more people still in their earthly bodies, it's the same but add quiet time together. Spiritual time together. Not searching for something outside of themselves but just learning to *be* together. To connect within that space which is spirit.

So there's no need to get here any faster through suicide. It all works out the same in the end. All the lessons still need to be learned. Why make it harder for yourself and for those who love you?"

How Do I Live Here?

More than once, I felt I couldn't continue. The feelings were so raw.

"This is too much. I can't feel things this much, David. I'm so emotional. Too sensitive. I feel it all the time unless I block you out."

He just watched me, letting me ramble.

"What am I gonna do with this, David? What am I gonna do with you dead and me not? And I have to live here. Without you."

Finally, he spoke.

"You're going to live your life. Enjoy it. Love."

"How do I do that without you?"

"Know that it's real. I'm real. Still."

He never wavered. Never broke eye contact. "You're not without me."

"It's not the same." I hated to sound whiny. Hoped I didn't sound whiny.

I sure felt whiny.

"What happens if you shut me out? Shut out your light, your spirit?"

I shook my head. "I feel dead inside."

"Yeah." He nodded. "Because it's the light that makes you live."

"I'll never figure it all out. You've tried my whole life to teach me, and I can't get it. If when we die, we migrate towards groups of the same spiritual development, I'll never be with you!" I shook my head and looked down, unwilling to allow him a glimpse of the forming tears.

But he knew.

"Oh, yes you will. You are with me now. And listen, you're ahead of me, anyway. You're physical, and you already have this stuff figured out. You know and understand more of how it all works before you're even completely here!"

"But I don't know how to live here," I told him.

"Here's the secret. Well, it's not really a secret because it's open to everyone if they'll just hear it. Allow both your physical self and your spiritual self to live simultaneously. Your spirit should lead and all that you know and that is present there should and will be reflected in your physical. Totally. Total immersion. Focus on your spirit. That's who you are. Focus on your joy and where you find it, within, and allow that joy to lead you in how you live your life…the things you do, the relationships you keep.

"Your spiritual and your physical must be true to each other. Strip away the external and find who you are. And then live."

I knew what he meant. Feel it, let the emotion guide me, share it with others. Find what activity provides the same feeling and express that emotion through that activity where it will be nurtured and grow. Understanding helped me feel better almost immediately. I knew what I wanted to do.

"I want to write about all of this."

"You should."

"I'm not sure how I should write it." I'm in middle America. Could I admit to anyone just how different my life and beliefs are?

He looked at me, confused. "You should write it as it is."

"But how will people best accept it? Should it be fiction? Non-fiction? I've asked Mike and Megan, and I think they're just leaving it up to me."

David laughed. "Because it's your story."

I grinned, loving his laugh, loving the way he still could tease me, that he did still tease me. "I just," I paused. "I just don't know what people will think."

"Why do you care?"

I shrugged. "More and more near death experiences are being written about, and if it was like that then I suppose I wouldn't hesitate. Well, not much," I added as I saw his eyebrows raise. He knew me too well. "This isn't a near death experience, though. Instead, it's a life experience. I wonder if I should stop being scared of telling people the truth and just call it a true life experience. It is, in essence, the fullness of life, of truly living." I glanced up at him and saw his smile, his eyes flashing. He nodded slightly so I'd continue. "The point is, we can connect to this heaven, this spiritual life, not only when we die but also while we still reside within our physical bodies."

Still, he nodded. And smiled. I continued with no hesitation. I knew what needed to be said. What I needed to do. "This is because despite the fact that our spirits are in fact encased in a physical body, we are still spirit, and a spirit's home is heaven. While in our bodies, our 'job' is to bring heaven to earth and teach people who they are and that they too are the same and can do the same."

"What else?" David reached for my hand, remembered he couldn't take it, and pulled back. I watched him take a deep breath and realized it wasn't a breath of life but a breath of thought.

"It's my journey. I'm sharing my journey. I don't have to do anything to tell people. I can just be. It's okay to just be."

"I would hug you if I could."

"I know you would."

"Close your eyes, baby. Listen to me with your heart."

I closed my eyes and let all thoughts slide out of my head. I felt the swelling in my heart, felt his arms around me. "I love you," I heard him say in my head. "This love, it's who we are. It's who you are. It's not limited to us. I can just help you understand how it feels, what it is, where it comes from, what to do with it.

"Live this love, Julie. Be this love.

"That's how you fulfill your purpose. Understand?"

Eyes still closed, I nodded.

"Good."

I felt his arms wrap tighter around me, and I imagined pressing myself closer to him. With that memory, a wave of pain washed over me, but I shook off the grief before it enveloped me.

He wasn't my strength, my love, my joy. I was.

It was all in me just as it's in everyone. Find someone who knows that, too, and the feeling seems exponential. If you don't, that's okay, too. Nothing takes away from who you are or the amount of love you are.

The Best We Could

In a dream, I floated across a field, over a river, drawn to the glowing light. David. I reached him and became immersed in his light.

It was like our energy needed to be together...needed to mingle, to touch, to entwine. Magnets - positive and negative.

"You were always the positive," I told him.

"Don't say that."

"It's true."

"Julie."

"What?" I lifted my eyebrows at him, daring him to say something, praying he'd say something... He brushed a knuckle across my cheek and shook his head. Deep in the dream, I could feel his touch, and I leaned against him.

"I wish it had been different." I whispered. Afraid. He might think it silly. I shouldn't admit it. It was the wrong thing to feel. The wrong way to be. "I don't know," I continued. "I just don't understand why I found you when it was too late. Why feel the way I felt about you when it was wrong to do anything about it?"

I glanced up at him finding his eyes, watching him. He looked at me, and for the first time since I'd seen his spirit, he had that contemplative look, kind of confused, unsure. I hadn't seen that on him in a very long time. "I've gone over it too many times. People get married for all kinds of reasons. Sometimes, we just don't know how it really feels, how it's supposed to feel, being married to someone. We don't understand the depth of it. It doesn't mean we've done anything wrong or can't love or can't make a joyful life…it's just not the same. I didn't know. I never knew I could feel the way I felt with you. I got married and did all the right things. I tried to keep doing the right things long after I met you but in the end, I couldn't. I didn't know what to do, didn't want to hurt her. Didn't want to hurt you.

"So I hurt. And I'll take that although I wished more than once that I'd hurt her instead. I'm not proud of that."

He shook his head. "I just couldn't do it, though. I suppose that's right." He laughed, a low, this-isn't-really-funny-but-I'll-make-fun-of-myself laugh. "The right thing to do. I always did the right thing."

"So did I," I answered.

He nodded. "Until me."

I couldn't deny that.

"What have we done?" I asked him. "David, what did we do?"

"We did the best we could," he told me. "The best we could. That's all we could do."

"But I wanted more," I whispered.

He reached for me, but I couldn't feel his hand touching me anymore, could only see it, the light of it shimmering next to me. I remembered how it felt when he touched me, and the weight of it all gripped my heart and squeezed. I briefly thought what I'd thought many times before. Maybe I couldn't survive all of this after all.

We had done the best we could. Still, we were doing the best we could. And I don't mean the best we could with excuses, not then or now…not the kind where you half-ass the job and then say well, it was the best I could…no, instead truly the best…the best we have to offer at the time we're living it, the best from deep inside… we do the best we can. That's the most any of us can ever do.

Another Little Lost Girl

"Hey!"

I roll over and look at my phone in the dark. 4:45 a.m.

Ugh.

"Seriously, can't you wait until after 6:00 at least? Ever?"

I hear his laugh. "You're distracted then."

There's probably some truth to that.

He's persistent. As always. "I want you to see this. Close your eyes."

"And sleep?" I have to give him a little bit of a hard time, right?

He rolls his eyes and grins at me. "Close your eyes."

In the movie screen of my mind, I see a little girl. She stands at a wooden rail fence looking out at acres of pasture land. I guess she's about ten. She has black wavy hair and wears high waisted jeans with a tucked in white shirt. The girl watches a man on a horse riding through the pasture. I can feel the love she has for him. It fills my abdomen, my upper belly, my chest and wants to burst forth from me. I understand that this is how much she loves.

The man rides closer, and I see his face. It's my granddad, my stepmother's father.

A new scene replaces the old. A family sits eating dinner. I see the girl again only this time she's older, maybe in her mid-teens. Lots of conversation, lots of laughter. There's love and respect in the way they talk to each other - the girl, her brother, her mother, her father. They're good people. Kind, hard-working, happy.

New scene. Not too many years later. The girl stands at her brother's grave. She doesn't cry then, but she has been. It's time to move past that. Crying won't help anyone else right now. She tightens her heart just a little bit. There's too much to do to let her emotions stop her.

I see the girl again. More time has passed, but I'm not sure how much. Maybe five more years. She's a young woman. She sits on the edge of her bed staring at a picture she grips tightly. I feel her grief. Her loss. Her mom is dead. She feels so lost.

She breathes deeply, stands up, and sets the picture on the nightstand. Brushing the pleats down on her slacks, she holds herself a little taller and tightens her heart just a tiny bit more. There are things to do.

Quickly more scenes passed - the girl, a woman now, at her husband's funeral, her three small children gathered around her all trying to hold her hand, pressing themselves up tightly against her. Only a few years after that, standing with my dad in our living room. I see her with her fists pressed against her mouth, sadness and grief in her eyes. Dad has his hand on her shoulder. She's just received the news her father has been killed in a work accident. My dad barely catches her as she crumples to the floor.

The images shake me. While I knew my stepmother had suffered multiple losses and that it had to have affected her, I'd never before witnessed these scenes, never felt the grief and hopelessness she felt.

"Now feel this." David's voice breaks through to me. I clear my mind and stare at a black empty screen. I focus not on what I can see but how I feel.

Determination fills me. I stand (figuratively) strong. I will take care of this. I'll take care of my children. Me. I'll do what it takes to create my life. Practical. Down to business. There are things to do.

A quick moment of feeling out of control flits by. So many things have been out of my control. I feel helpless. I hate that feeling and will not let it take hold in my life.

"I understand that feeling." I whisper to David, not wanting to break the feel of it all.

He nods.

"Now, I want you to think about this. Remember the anger you felt?"

"Yes."

"The bitterness?"

"Yes."

"The need for control your entire life but especially when you felt helpless in your grief?"

I nodded. I knew where he was going, and I wasn't sure I wanted to hear it.

"How do you react when those feelings overcome you? When others aren't as expected? Or how you think they should be?"

I just lay there. I didn't want to answer.

"You're kind of like her." He tells me this, and it makes me angry. Not with him but with myself.

"No, I'm not." I argue. "I'm not spiteful and mean. I'm not hateful like that. I'm not her."

"Shh." He comforts me, and I feel his embrace. "No, you're not spiteful and mean. But you can be. We all can be. How do you treat people who make you feel out of control? Outwardly or inwardly? How do you feel at those moments? What do you say? How do you react?"

I didn't answer him. I was absorbing what I knew was the truth, no matter how much I hated it. From his words, I could imagine further - a hard-working, loving, happy woman who'd lost her entire family. Determined to make the best of her life, she moved forward. But we never quite lose all of that underlying bitterness, do we? And if keeping things in order in our lives helps us cope, how do we interact with and react to people who rock that control, who don't act in a way we're used to, whom we don't understand? That shakes up our perceived perfect world we've made for ourselves.

"Give her a break. She's always done the best she could, too. She still does."

In that moment, my anger towards my stepmother dissipated. I understood.

I forgave her because I finally 'got it'. And I forgave myself for always thinking it had been about me.

Religion

David always taught me...from the parking lot and discussions about the different kinds of love, to the Tower at Six Flags talking about faith, to the long drives and discussions about being compelled to do something rather than remain stagnant. It made sense to me that he continued to teach me after his physical death. Why wouldn't he? Our connection wasn't lost. I knew that now. Nothing would ever break it. Sure, we might have stretched it and pulled way apart but when we spiritually needed each other it snapped back together as a rubber band might. No bond of unconditional love is truly ever broken.

I worried for a long time whether my experiences negated my religion, or vice versa. I've come to realize that religion actually is a great in-between when we're looking for more, when we first understand that we are more than just our physical bodies. Religion can get us on the right track to knowing God.

Quite a few years ago, I began to hear people talk about having a 'personal relationship with Christ'. These people had begun to understand their religion encompassed more than just the rules and that by making it personal they could begin to see the divine within themselves. They still attribute that divine to Christ and that's okay. Saying it's Christ or saying it's not…those things don't matter because they're really both right. The 'personal relationship' is a step in the right direction. Those who begin to live this way are beginning to 'get it'.

While still dealing with the internal conflict between religion and spirituality (for lack of better descriptions), one of my friends said, "Oh, be careful. You can't always trust that; it could be an evil spirit." That caused me worry for a little while, but I prayed about it and opened up my Bible.

The page fell open to Matthew 7:17 (7-17 is the date David died, by the way) which reads, *Likewise, every good tree bears good fruit, but a bad tree bears bad fruit.*

That made total sense and provided the comfort I needed. My experiences were all 'good trees'. They brought peace and comfort, hope and joy to me. These are things we all strive for and they all come from God, from goodness. From these good things, more good things are born. No evil comes from something so truly joyous.

I've come to learn that religion, rather than always be a path towards God, tends to make us look outside of ourselves to find Him. That keeps us separate from the Divine when in fact, we are one with it. We're given all we need to be whole. We are all we need.

Facing Fear

The feeling of David came over me, and I knew he was with me. Somehow. I couldn't see him, but just as we recognize someone's energy and spirit when they are physically with us, so too can we recognize a passed loved one's energy and spirit.

"Hi," I whispered. I could have said it in my head, but sometimes I feel it necessary to make our communication tangible. Not that words are tangible, but they are more so than thoughts. At least, that's how it feels.

The energy of his smile filled me and wrapped around me, and I was comforted by the joy I felt. It never quit amazing me how I felt so much the same with him in spirit as I did with him in the physical.

"You can hear me." He stated rather than asked. Just making sure I was awake, I think.

I nodded.

"We're talking about fear today." I peeked my eyes open hoping to see him, but I only saw blank space.

"I can't see you." It seemed important that I see him at that moment.

His thoughts came quickly. "You don't need to. I want you to feel this. I want you learn this. Trust this. It's part of overcoming fear."

Carefully, I listened. I wanted to protest. Just because I wanted to see him didn't mean I was afraid not to. Did it?

Yes, it probably did. I needed to see him to know he was there. I still held the fear I made him up. I was crazy, like my mother. I'm sorry, Mom. I love you. But I don't want to be crazy.

I wanted to see him, but even though I didn't trust myself to hear and understand everything, I did trust David. I understood what he wanted me to do. And be.

I nodded again. "I'm listening."

Thoughts rushed in again. "What holds you back from being all you're designed to be? Fear. What are you afraid of? You're not good enough? Smart enough? Faithful enough? Enough? Others won't like you? They'll make fun of you? Judge you? Criticize you?

"Fear immobilizes a person. It causes them to shrivel into a shell of what they might possibly be. It keeps them from learning who they truly are. It causes them to falter. It keeps them from living fully and boldly.

"But you know this, you know you are more than this physical world. The light isn't just in you. It is you. You are an equal part of the Divine light that is considered God, source, universe. No more and no less than anyone else. You are perfect as you are and just because others don't understand doesn't make it any less so.

"By knowing your light, yourself, there's no need or room for any of those fears. They don't matter. Once you shed them, you can step out into your life and know contentment in all you are and all you do.

"So many people live in fear. It causes greed, anger, unhappiness, pettiness, insecurity. All of these things keep them from love which keeps them from peace and joy. Live true to yourself in your love and fear won't affect you."

Fear has held me back from living my life completely in the way I've wanted to. I'm ready to let it go.

Negativity

Negative energy flows in and out like a gentle but steady wave. It generates within ourselves and that energy is the only energy that we have control over. The negativity that originates from others only belongs to them. It is not our job to take it on, to allow it to mingle and merge with our own. We can only control our own energy, and that's not done by single moment episodic attempts to dispel negative energy. It comes from consciously working to move negative energy out of ourselves and breathe positive energy in.

As difficult as it can be to be around those who radiate negativity, it is only through building our own defenses that we can stop allowing them to affect us. Through meditation and prayer, quiet time and reflection, we can purposely and intentionally fill ourselves with positive. Pack the positive in so that instead of the external negativity infusing our own systems, there's just no room for it. It can only touch on the edges of our positive barrier we've erected and so it can never take purchase and invade. Instead, hanging on the edge, it becomes easy for us to shuff it off and out and once again allow positivity to reign.

This is the secret to dealing with our own negative thoughts and tendencies and in dealing with others who convey negativity. In these ways, we can allow love to fill us and continue to drive us in all we do despite what those around us are doing or saying.

What Now?

Dusk came, the sun resting gently at the top of the trees before it made that final plunge leaving us in darkness instead of with the orange streaks that still provided us with a bit of light.

Mike sat beside me on the porch, swinging his feet slowly back and forth. I looked carefully at him, studying the side of his face, thinking how well I knew him. How could I not after more than 20 years of living with him, sleeping next to him.

I loved him so much. Through so many years, I let my fears and insecurities keep me from loving him completely. Now, I understood that my love can never be limited by anything other than my failure to recognize it and to let it shine.

I thought back over the last so many years. I considered the questions I'd had, the wonder why I'd married him, the frustration I'd felt because he wasn't the way I thought he should be. I remembered my anger with him sometimes directly and most often indirectly and how it had affected our relationship time and time again. I'd been so angry, and really he'd never been anything different than he'd been from the start.

In fact, because he loved me, his differences were for the better. They were for me. I understood that now.

I struggled for many years. With what could have been. What never was. What never would be.

I spent my lifetime not doing all I wanted to do or saying what I wanted to say because it wasn't the 'right' thing to do or say. According to whom? Fictional critics, products of my own imagination.

As I cried myself to sleep night after night, Mike stayed steady. He never rushed me. Never told me not to grieve.

He didn't always know what to do or say, but he never let me doubt he was there for me.

Throughout the years, I transitioned from convenient faith to faith in religion's God to the magnitude of the true God and the spirit who resides in me. Everything had to happen as it did or my analytical mind would never have truly accepted it. I would have always wanted it, but I wouldn't have known it.

This journey continues, and I look forward to hearing what else David has to teach me. Because of him, my relationships feel fuller now – with Mike, my kids, my parents and family and friends. My life has become exciting again as I see the wonder in each tiny moment. I understand and appreciate we are all in different places along the path of our relationships with God, with ourselves, and each other. We are each our own person, and my job is not to change someone else but to love them and accept them and let my own light shine as brightly as it can.

Prayer has become my everything. It's my connection with spirit and my true self. I'm thrilled with the idea of all the possibilities opened up to me by knowing that I am love. I'm grateful, humbled, amazed.

I've found it all inside of me - complete in spirit, with my family, loving David - not separate but a part of me. A part of all the love that is God.

I'm often compelled to move within this love and find ways I can share it. Other times, I prefer to just be. I can sit and listen to the rain, walk through the garden feeling the energy of the plants, meditate for hours strengthening my spiritual connection, and it's all good.

There's no way I *should* be any more. Nothing I *must* do. Just sometimes things I *want* to do. Think of those possibilities when we discover our light. Just think. Thank. Live. Love.

Be you.

You're enough.

The Best We Could

About the Author

Julie Richmond found inspiration and motivation through God's amazing grace after the death of her best friend. Through her grief journey, she finally realized her incredible light within. Realizing that others don't always know that light is in them, too, Julie set out to share her experiences so that everyone might understand.

While describing herself as a 'work in progress', Julie wakes each day determined not to let fear keep her from living her life fully and boldly, pursuing her dreams, and loving each and every one of God's incredible creations.

Julie currently lives in the Midwest with her husband, three children, and granddaughter. She's been a teacher for almost 25 years (and is sure that means she started teaching at the age of 12 since she just couldn't be that old). She has a degree in Communications (talking!) with a minor in English and both master's and specialist degrees in Educational Administration.

Connect Online:

The Best We Could on Facebook:
http://on.fb.me/1CZErGy

Email: findinggodcreatingme@gmail.com